Love Me Tonight

OXFORD GUIDES TO FILM MUSICALS

Dominic Broomfield-McHugh, Series Editor

Love Me Tonight
Geoffrey Block

Singin' in the Rain
Andrew Buchman

La La Land
Hannah Lewis

Love Me Tonight

GEOFFREY BLOCK

OXFORD
UNIVERSITY PRESS

Oxford University Press is a department of the University of Oxford.
It furthers the University's objective of excellence in research, scholarship,
and education by publishing worldwide. Oxford is a registered trade mark of
Oxford University Press in the UK and in certain other countries.

Published in the United States of America by Oxford University Press
198 Madison Avenue, New York, NY 10016, United States of America.

Library of Congress Cataloging-in-Publication Data
Names: Block, Geoffrey Holden, 1948– author.
Title: Love me tonight / Geoffrey Block.
Description: New York : Oxford University Press, 2024. |
Series: Oxford guides to film musicals series | Includes bibliographical references and index. |
Identifiers: LCCN 2024022574 (print) | LCCN 2024022575 (ebook) |
ISBN 9780197566183 (hardback) | ISBN 9780197566190 (paperback) |
ISBN 9780197566213 (epub) | ISBN 9780197566220 |
Subjects: LCSH: Love me tonight (Motion picture) |
Musical films—United States—History and criticism.
Classification: LCC PN1997.L766 B56 2024 (print) | LCC PN1997.L766 (ebook) |
DDC 791.43/72—dc23/eng/20240529
LC record available at https://lccn.loc.gov/2024022574
LC ebook record available at https://lccn.loc.gov/2024022575

DOI: 10.1093/9780197566220.001.0001

Paperback printed by Marquis Book Printing, Canada
Hardback printed by Bridgeport National Bindery, Inc., United States of America

To my beloved mother-in-law
LUCILLE KULWIN (1928–2019)
Mother to Jacqueline
"Grandma Lucy" to Jessamyn and Eli
Who enriched our lives immeasurably with her love, warmth, and caring

Contents

Contents

Illustrations

Musical Examples

Figures

Tables

Series Editor's Foreword

When Paramount's *Love Me Tonight* was released in August 1932, it drew ecstatic coverage from the press, including *The Hollywood Reporter*:

> The exhibitor readers of the reviews in these columns and you of Hollywood who maintain interest in its picture reports, will hardly believe that the Paramount picture, "Love Me Tonight," starring Maurice Chevalier, is as fine a picture, as great an attraction and production as this reviewer will report. We say this, because in these times of stress, of cost-saving and bad business, hardly any studio would take the time to go to the enormous expense of modelling such a picture, the very QUALITY of which resulted in our opinion.[1]

The reviewer goes on to praise the film's all-round excellence, which it attributed to the performance of star Chevalier ("a Maurice we have never seen before"), the direction of Rouben Mamoulian ("a veritable lesson in imagination for any director in this business"), the "catchy tunes" of Rodgers and Hart, and the screenplay.

These elements also form key elements of this revelatory study of the film by Geoffrey Block. One of the world's most prolific and distinguished authors of books and articles on musical theater, film, and beyond, Block adds to his earlier scholarship on Rodgers and Hart, beginning with *Enchanted Evenings* and followed by an indispensable monograph on Rodgers's musicals and *The Richard Rodgers Reader*—with a rich and illuminating study of how *Love Me Tonight* came to be and why it matters.[2] Block points out that while the film has long been revered by experts, it was rarely seen in the second half of the twentieth century, its release in home video format (in this case, DVD) being postponed until 2003. The movie remains obscure to the public at large compared to, say, *The Wizard of Oz* (1939) from the same period.

Yet Rodgers himself wrote of it as "among the most imaginative screen musicals ever made,"[3] and most, if not quite all, commentators have put its brilliance and originality on a pedestal alongside better-known classics such as *Singin' in the Rain* (1952), another film covered in Oxford *Guides to Film Musicals*. The most consistently admired element is Mamoulian's direction, which forms the focus of Block's insightful opening chapter. Meticulously examining multiple drafts of the screenplay, Block charts Mamoulian's role in designing the script "to show off the versatility and range of two major stars Maurice Chevalier and Jeanette MacDonald, [and] to integrate the stellar songs created by composer Rodgers and lyricist Lorenz Hart."

Those eight songs form the focus of the second chapter, in which Block presents a thorough and comprehensive analysis of "the dramatic contexts, what's going on in the lyrics and music, how story, words, and music work together . . . and the extent to which they are integrated into the fabric of the film." A highlight of both the movie and the chapter is the "passed-along song" "Isn't It Romantic?," an extensive sequence in which one of Rodgers and Hart's most popular songs is adopted by a series of different characters who symbolically carry the song from Chevalier's Parisian tailor shop to the country castle of his lover, played by MacDonald.

The balance of Block's book is devoted to an enlightening chapter on Rodgers's music for the whole film, including an imaginative instrumental score heard under the dialogue (unusually, Rodgers was asked to write this in addition to the songs), to a chapter on the role of censorship in shaping the film in which Mamoulian skillfully manages to challenge and circumvent the censorship imposed by the Production Code. The final chapter focuses on the movie's unusual critical and popular reception.

In that final section, Block notes that "a significant fact in the reception of *Love Me Tonight* is the fact that it inspired an impressive array of influential makers of film musicals in the 1940s and 1950s," including Vincente Minnelli, Charles Walters, and Stanley Donen. In turn, Block's important volume promises to inspire readers and scholars with its breathtaking array of insights and revelations on a true Hollywood classic.

Dominic Broomfield-McHugh

Series Editor

Oxford Guides to Film Musicals

Preface

"*Love Me Tonight* is a wonderful film, one of the two or three of the
greatest musicals *ever* made."

Richard Barrios (1995)

The purpose of this volume in the series Oxford Guides to Film Musicals is to
introduce scholars, students, and general readers to *Love Me Tonight* (1932),
a musical film fairy tale that has enjoyed high stature but remains less familiar
than other acknowledged classics. According to some critics such as Richard
Barrios and Jeanine Basinger, this seemingly simple fable of love between a
princess and a tailor is a great work of art. As the history presented here will
show, the techniques pioneered in this early sound film have influenced gen-
erations of major filmmakers, but the film remains loved and appreciated
even for the style and imagination with which these techniques are used, the
integration of a superb screenplay and superb music, the consistently fine
acting, and a subtle and stylish combination of comedy, sex, and romance.
The Guide will devote individual chapters to the work's major contributors,
its genesis and the development of the screenplay, the songs, the instrumental
numbers, the role censorship has played in the history of the film, and the
film's reception from its time to ours. All of these topics will be informed by
extensive archival resources located in major library collections as well as the
indispensable resources housed at the Paramount Studio archive.

  Love Me Tonight was released both on VHS and DVD in 2003. This milestone occurred considerably later than the release of other classic movies,
some of which were released soon after VHS technology arrived in the late
1970s. Unfortunately in my case, this commercial unveiling coincided with
rather than preceded the publication of my book on the film's composer,
Richard Rodgers.[1] Before this annus mirabilis I had read the published literature about the film, but like many film enthusiasts had only seen portions
of it, most memorably the film montage of the famous "passed-along" or
"traveling" song "Isn't It Romantic?" in which a melody begun in Maurice
Chevalier's Parisian tailor's shop eventually made its way to Princess Jeanette
MacDonald's country chateau.[2] I had also seen film clips on television of

"Lover," the song Jeanette sings to her horse with lyrics that would likely have been censored had they been directed to the ears of a human lover, and portions of "The Hunt" ballet.

Having seen only a small but tantalizing percentage of the total film, I read with great interest the detail its proud composer Rodgers (1902–1979) lavished on this film musical in his autobiography *Musical Stages*.[3] Created with his lyricist Lorenz Hart (1895–1943), it certainly ranks as their best (but to be accurate, perhaps only) remembered Hollywood adventure from the early years of sound cinema, 1931 to 1935.[4] Highly enthusiastic commentaries and assessments in books on Rodgers and Hart, Rouben Mamoulian (1898–1987), and surveys of musical film have followed the film since its debut. In 1965, the film critic Leonard Maltin unflinchingly concluded that *Love Me Tonight* is "one of the best musicals *ever* made" [italics mine].[5] More than fifty years later, a magisterial history of the Hollywood musical from *The Jazz Singer* (1927) to *La La Land* (2016) by noted film historian Jeanine Basinger that appeared in 2019 unequivocally states that *Love Me Tonight* "has never really been surpassed for its integration of music, plot, and character."[6] More than ninety years after its debut in 1932 *Love Me Tonight* remains as revered as ever.

Given this critical esteem from major voices in the field, it seems all the more striking that *Love Me Tonight* remains far less well known than such critically praised original film musicals as *Singin' in the Rain* (1952), *Gigi* (1958), or *Mary Poppins* (1964). Almost invariably when I informed friends and students that I was writing a book on *Love Me Tonight*, the title of this widely heralded film, as well as the name of its director, drew a blank. The people in this admittedly limited sample often remembered Maurice Chevalier well from *Gigi*. Many were familiar with Rodgers and Hart's "Isn't It Romantic?" in various contexts (including its use in other movies such as *Sabrina*). Everyone knew the trilogy of memorable *stage* works Mamoulian directed after *Love Me Tonight* (*Porgy and Bess*, *Oklahoma!*, and *Carousel*), even if they had not associated these milestones with Mamoulian. But for many, *Love Me Tonight* fell below the radar. In short, the process of writing this book has persuaded me that *Love Me Tonight* is one film masterpiece that could use an introduction.

The relative obscurity of *Love Me Tonight* stands in sharp contrast to the legacy of *The Wizard of Oz* (1939) and another durable survivor from the 1930s, the first full-length Disney film, *Snow White and the Seven Dwarfs* (1937). Unlike *The Wizard* and *Snow White*, most film musicals that debuted in the 1930s, including *Love Me Tonight*, remained largely unseen until the 1980s or later. I was lucky to have spent my formative years in or near college towns where I could view my first Astaire and Rogers films at special festivals in the 1970s and 1980s, before they eventually became widely available on VHS, DVD, and YouTube, but I don't recall *Love Me Tonight* being shown on these occasions.

Although the general public may be unfamiliar with *Love Me Tonight* as a *film*, at least three songs, "Isn't It Romantic?," "Lover," and "Love Me Tonight," soon gained admission to the Great American Songbook and renown via popular recordings like Peggy Lee's provocative jazzy 1952 version of "Lover," which no one could misinterpret as a song originally intended for a horse. Eventually, but not until 2001, the four songs commercially recorded by Chevalier or MacDonald in 1932 became available on CD: "Isn't It Romantic?" (MacDonald), "Mimi" (Chevalier), "The Poor Apache" (Chevalier), and "Love Me Tonight" (MacDonald).[7] "Isn't It Romantic?" and "Lover," the latter not recorded by MacDonald but widely known from a hit release performed by bandleader Paul Whiteman (with one chorus sung by Jack Fulton), were among the most popular songs of their day and remain so in ours.

Through the quirky taste of record producer Ben Bagley in his *Rodgers and Hart Revisited Vol. 3*, I also became familiar with a recording of "The Man for Me" (a.k.a. "The Letter Song"), a song deleted from the finished film and which remains unpublished.[8] I was unaware of the long- out-of-print LP reissue that includes these songs and others directly taken from the film soundtrack in 1932: "That's the Song of Paree," "Lover," "Mimi" (in a track that offered some dialogue called "Roadside Scene"), "A Woman Needs Something," "The Poor Apache," and "Love Me Tonight."[9] Some of these song rarities would remain for the most part unheard, and certainly not readily seen, until the film's 2003 release.

Although there are a few dissenters, most notably film critic Andrew Sarris in the 1960s and 1970s, the magnitude and virtual unanimity of critical praise bestowed on *Love Me Tonight* is nothing short of overwhelming.[10] Future commentators largely shared the high opinion of *Love Me Tonight* that Rodgers expressed in *Musical Stages*, including his pronouncement that this film "is still considered to be among the most imaginative screen musicals *ever* made" [italics mine].[11] One of the questions this volume will attempt to answer is why *Love Me Tonight* enjoys such lofty critical stature and what makes this film so memorably sui generis as well as an exemplar of a familiar film genre, the fairy tale musical.

While this Guide does not ignore the many notable cinematic aspects of this film that have been so ably explored by film scholars, it will allow far more space to discuss the musical, literary, and dramatic dimensions that have received less emphasis in previous film studies. Just as music historians with their rich musical discussions have added a new dimension to the valuable commentary offered by theater historians and critics about stage musicals, a central purpose of this volume will be to add a musical emphasis intended to shed new light on why *Love Me Tonight* merits this kind of scholarly as well as critical attention and respect. Like future books in this series, this volume on *Love Me Tonight* will take advantage of a rich array of archival resources, in this case the extensive Rouben Mamoulian and Richard Rodgers collections in the Library of Congress, the indispensable film archives held at Paramount Studios and the Margaret Herrick Library in Los Angeles, and the Richard Rodgers Papers in the New York Public Library.

The first chapter of this Guide, "Introducing the Major Players and Developing the Screenplay for a Fairy Tale Musical," will tell the story of how *Love Me Tonight* came to be, starting with the search to find a film property for Maurice Chevalier, how Mamoulian came to be unexpectedly hired to replace Ernst Lubitsch, and Mamoulian's meeting with the French playwright Léopold Marchand at a party. From the beginning, Mamoulian saw the intrinsic musicality of this story based on a play by Marchand and Paul Armont called *Le tailleur au chateau (The Tailor in the Castle)* and designed a musical with music at its center. Using treatments and screenplay drafts in the Mamoulian Collection housed in the Library of Congress, the first chapter will trace the initial creation and evolution of key dramatic events, plot developments, and character transformations from the incomplete and sometimes tenuous first outlines and treatments to the final screenplay. The chapter will also critically examine the reasons behind the decisions Mamoulian and his screenwriters made as they gradually placed the songs.

Chapter 2, "Songs by Rodgers and Hart," focuses on the lyrics and music of all the songs in *Love Me Tonight* and the role these songs play within their dramatic contexts, their reprises, and how a wide variety of song types and purposes (divided equally between diegetic and nondiegetic) relate to and enhance the film's drama and visual realization. The chapter will also take a look at the duet "The Man for Me," which was sung and filmed but removed before the film's release.

A second chapter on the music, "Rodgers the Musical 'Auteur': Instrumental Numbers, Leitmotivs, Borrowings, Allusions, and Underscoring" (chapter 3), considers all the music other than the songs. Mamoulian's unusual idea of building a screenplay around a group of songs rather than the reverse was matched by his equally unusual, if not unprecedented, request that Rodgers also compose the instrumental numbers, especially the "Hunt" ballet, music for specific characters (leitmotivs), and underscoring (music underneath dialogue), rather than assigning these tasks to a studio staff arranger or composer.

Chapter 4, "Sex and Censorship," will discuss the history, principles, and influence of the Studio Relations Committee during *Love Me Tonight*'s creation and first release in 1932 before the introduction of severe film censorship, and its rerelease in 1949, when the Production Code Administration insisted on the removal of several conversations about the "Virgin's Spring," the innuendo-rich "A Woman Needs Something Like That," and about fifteen seconds of Myrna Loy singing a reprise of "Mimi" in a diaphanous nightgown. The chapter will use the extensive paper trail of memos between Paramount executives and PCA enforcers to explore the reasons behind the censors' choices and the impact of these decisions, particularly those imposed upon the film's rerelease. Although intrusive, the silver lining behind these cuts is that the amount of film material challenged in 1932 and destroyed in 1949 was far less than usually cited, probably a few minutes at most. Far more significant was what made it *past* the Code, both in 1932 and 1949.

The final chapter, "The Reception of *Love Me Tonight* from Its Time to Ours" (chapter 5), tries to explain how a critically well-regarded but unprofitable movie gradually evolved into a timeless classic. The chapter will explore what critics and future directors liked about the movie in its time and since, and it will try to make sense of the dissonance between the astonishing acclaim it has received in film histories and its relative public obscurity until its belated resurfacing on DVD in 2003. Hugh Fordin was on to something when he wrote that the film's director, Mamoulian, "is part of the lives of millions of people who have never heard of him."[12] Unlike most moviegoers, directors like Vincente Minnelli, Charles Walters, and Stanley Donen *did* know Mamoulian's work, particularly *Love Me Tonight*, and were inspired by it. They also learned from Mamoulian's great directorial achievement with its superb score, well-constructed screenplay, top-notch acting ensemble, striking camera work, and invariably attractive and stylish art direction.

Love Me Tonight also contains moments of humor destined to appeal to viewers of any age or era. As with many stage and film comedies of the 1930s, the humor is often verbal, most quotably when Valentine, when asked if she can "go for a doctor" replies, "Certainly. Bring him right in." Still more often it is the camera that amuses us, particularly in Mamoulian's use of extreme camera speeds, fast or slow. Prominent examples of the latter include the Duke's slow motion bridge game played to the accompaniment of "There'll Be a Hot Time in the Old Town Tonight" ("à la dirge") and the scene at the end of the hunt where the horses of the Duke's entourage tiptoe away from Maurice's cabin in silence and slow motion so as not to disturb the stag he has rescued. A particularly memorable comic moment occurs during the uproar set off by the revelation that Maurice is "nothing but a tailor" when an agitated Aunt knocks over a vase, an action that sets off an exaggerated explosive sound, followed by successive yapping sounds barked by all three Aunts that culminate with a close-up of a little dog with an identical yap.

In the end, Marchand and Armont's delightful tale of the tailor and the princess came true on the screen. The passed-along song that takes "Isn't It Romantic?" on a complex journey through montage, starting in Maurice's tailor shop and eventually finding its way to Princess Jeanette's castle balcony, poses the question. Approximately ninety minutes later we know the answer is a resounding "Yes."

Acknowledgments

Special thanks go to my dear friend and colleague, Dominic Broomfield-McHugh, who conceived the idea for Oxford Guides to Film Musicals, for which he serves as series editor. Dominic also invited me to write this volume, for which he offered unceasing enthusiasm, support, and encouragement as well as astute and helpful editing and guidance at every stage. And without the leadership, expertise, and goodwill of Oxford's Norm Hirschy, this promising new series simply would not have happened. Thanks as well to all those at Oxford University Press who provided the invaluable professional support necessary to successfully shepherd this volume into print, in particular my helpful as well as extremely capable production team: Joellyn Ausanka (copy-editor); Zara Cannon-Mohammed (project editor); and Bridget M. Austiguy-Preschel (project manager).

I would also like to thank another dear friend and colleague, Andrew Buchman, who took the time to gather and prepare for my us Rodgers's musical sketches and scores and Hart's lyric drafts located at the Library of Congress and the New York Library. In addition to this act of collegiality and friendship, Andrew doubled as a tireless sounding board who provided scrupulous and invariably helpful readings. I am truly in his debt. Many thanks also to Eli Block, who again supplied the professional and elegant typesetting of the music examples.

Special thanks for the generous services offered by the University of Puget Sound staff: Nic Casey, Digital Media Specialist, and Sara Johnson and Henry Waymack, at the Print and Copy Services, for preparing the photographs; Lori Ricigliano, Research Librarian at Collins Library, who tracked down Marchand and Armont's play *Le tailleur au château* shortly before it entered the public domain in the nick of time on January 1, 2020; and to the supportive library staff, Chris Dowd, Debbie Hill, and Cassandra Palmore.

Many thanks to the keepers of the voluminous and indispensable Rouben Mamouilian Collection held at the Library of Congress, which provided me with numerous treatments, screenplay drafts, and unpublished essays. The librarians at the Margaret Herrick Library in Los Angeles were also extremely helpful in providing their valuable materials, including *Love Me Tonight*'s final screenplay and the Production Code Files. Annie Killelea at Paramount Studios generously provided the handwritten score drafts and Conductor's Score, both of which were indispensable for the chapter "Rodgers the Musical 'Auteur.'"

Thanks also for the insightful comments and suggestions offered by Oxford's two outside reviewers. One of these reviewers identified himself as Joseph Horowitz, the author of the insightful *"On My Way": The Untold Story of Rouben Mamoulian, George Gershwin, and "Porgy and Bess,"* one among Horowitz's numerous books on American music. In addition, I am grateful to the many fine film scholars and critics (all duly acknowledged in the notes and bibliography) who paved the way for a musicologist to invade their turf. Finally, I want to express my deep gratitutde to my supportive and curious friends, colleagues, and students and to my endearing wife Jacqueline and our children, Jessamyn and Eli, who daily bestow meaning and joy to my work and my life.

1

Introducing the Major Players and Developing the Screenplay for a Fairy Tale Musical

GILBERT: How much can you loan me?

VALENTINE: (Hesitantly) Well, you know I'd gladly give you the shirt off my back—*She has turned a trifle, exposing the backless back, as she starts smoothing the gown over her hips.*

GILBERT: (After one look) Whom *did* you give it to?[1]

In the Beginning: Maurice Chevalier and Jeanette MacDonald

In his autobiography Richard Rodgers (1902–1979) gives the director Rouben Mamoulian (1898–1987) the main credit for crafting *Love Me Tonight* (1932). Five decades later, many critics continue to agree with Rodgers's 1975 assessment that Mamoulian's film ranks "among the most imaginative screen musicals ever made."[2] Although Rodgers expressed pride over his own contributions, he saw the result as a "Mamoulian film." Indeed, this chapter will mainly explore Mamoulian's role in the making of *Love Me Tonight*. It will tell the story of how Mamoulian supervised screenplay drafts designed to show off the versatility and range of two major stars, Maurice Chevalier and Jeanette MacDonald, to integrate the stellar songs created by composer Rodgers and lyricist Lorenz Hart (1895–1943) and the instrumental music and underscoring composed by Rodgers, and to explain why it is important as well as intrinsically interesting to know about the distinctive and unusual features of the creative process. After placing the songs and instrumental music within a workable dramatic context, Mamoulian, along with his screenwriters, Samuel Hoffenstein,[3] Waldemar Young,[4] and George Marion Jr.,[5] and later with his trusted art director Hans Dreier[6]

Love Me Tonight. Geoffrey Block, Oxford University Press. © Oxford University Press 2024.
DOI: 10.1093/9780197566220.003.0001

and cinematographer Victor Milner,[7] went on to create a musical film that not only Rodgers but numerous critics, historians, and film practitioners consider to be one of the outstanding film musicals of its, or, as some have proclaimed, any era.

Love Me Tonight may be a "Mamoulian film," but its genesis begins not with Mamoulian and those who assisted him but with Paramount's biggest musical film star at the time: Maurice Chevalier (1888–1972) (see Figure 1.1).

Figure 1.1 Rouben Mamoulian (left) and Maurice Chevalier (right).

The desire to give his many followers an opportunity to see Chevalier in a new picture was the film's raison d'être, and throughout its creation Paramount studio executives and their Pre-Production Code gatekeepers most often referred to *Love Me Tonight* as a "Chevalier picture." When the film was released, most reviewers took it for granted they were reviewing a new Chevalier movie rather than the latest film featuring the songwriters Rodgers and Hart and directed by Mamoulian. Between 1929 and 1934 Chevalier shared the screen with Jeanette MacDonald (1903–1965). The partnership of Chevalier and MacDonald was one of perhaps only three mega-star teams in the history of film musicals, alongside Fred Astaire and Ginger Rogers, who starred in nine dance musicals between 1933 and 1938 (a tenth would follow in 1949). The Philadelphia-born former operetta stage singer MacDonald partnered in *two* of these pairings, the first seemingly a counter-intuitive one with Chevalier, a self-taught Parisian cabaret singer, and later a more musically compatible partnership with the classically trained baritone from Providence, Rhode Island, Nelson Eddy (1901–1967).

During the five years of the Chevalier–MacDonald partnership, Ernst Lubitsch directed the first two of their four films, *The Love Parade* (1929) and *One Hour with You* (1932), and Mamoulian's *Love Me Tonight*, also from 1932, was the third. All three films were produced by Paramount. The final Chevalier–MacDonald collaboration, an adaptation of Franz Lehár's durable operetta *The Merry Widow* (1934), the only film among these continental fairy tales adapted from a stage work and the only film produced by MGM, was again directed by Lubitsch. As suggested by the appellation "a Chevalier picture," the Chevalier–MacDonald partnership was not an equal one, either at the box office or the studio payroll department. In the case of *Love Me Tonight*, according to Paramount's "Estimating Summary of Estimate Costs," Chevalier received $159,041.67 and MacDonald a relatively paltry $25,833.33.[8] The origins of this unequal status can be traced to Chevalier's phenomenal success in *Innocents of Paris*, which appeared shortly before *The Love Parade*, when Chevalier became "the first new superstar of the musical cinema."[9]

Considering their wide salary gap, it should not be surprising that in both *The Love Parade* and *One Hour with You* Chevalier received sole top billing, followed by the afterthought "with Jeanette MacDonald." As a partial redress of their disparate stature, MacDonald's lower ranking on the credits ladder was elevated in the latter film via the use of typeface equal in size. In the credits to *Love Me Tonight* Chevalier receives sole top billing and the largest type, but MacDonald's typeface is larger than that accorded the *other* co-stars. Only with *The Merry Widow* do the two stars appear in the same-size lettering and same credit slide, although Chevalier was visually elevated one notch above his co-star.

After *The Merry Widow,* the financially disappointing but critically acclaimed fourth pairing with MacDonald, Chevalier would virtually disappear from film musicals and Hollywood more generally. A quarter of a century later he returned in a featured role as the elderly boulevar-dier Honoré Lachailles singing "Thank Heaven for Little Girls" to open and close the film musical *Gigi* (1958).[10] In contrast to Chevalier's mete-oric but abbreviated film musical career, MacDonald, after showing off her comic flair (and too often for her taste in underwear as well), would enter a more successful, if somewhat humorless, second act alongside Eddy with *Naughty Marietta* in 1935, a debut followed by another six operettas, ending in 1942 with a film adaptation of Rodgers and Hart's 1938 stage musical *I Married an Angel*. In contrast to her films with Eddy, *Love Me Tonight* gave MacDonald the opportunity to demonstrate her dramatic as well as vocal and comic talents. The gender-bending plot even allowed the Princess to ride on horseback (allegedly without a stunt double), and after overcoming her class prejudices and falling madly in love with a "son-of-a-gun who is nothing but a tailor," subverts fairy tale protocol by allowing her to rescue the Prince rather than vice versa.

Chevalier and his better half (albeit at considerably less than half the salary) were both such bright stars, so irresistibly incompatible, and so well known that by 1932 they are identified in the film simply as Maurice and Jeanette. In addition, the film offered a cornucopia of accomplished comic actors and actresses in supporting roles, in particular Charlie Ruggles as Gilbert, Vicomte de Varèze, Charles Butterworth as the Count de Savignac, C. Aubrey Smith as the Duke D'Artelines, Elizabeth Patterson as the First Aunt, Ethel Griffies as the Second Aunt, and Robert Greig in his butling role as the Major Domo Flamand.[11] The film also made the most of Myrna Loy in a break-through comic role as the refreshingly forward Countess Valentine. Before the footage was removed, film audiences in 1932 even got to hear Loy sing for a few seconds for the first (and only) time in her long career in a re-prise of "Mimi."[12]

Enter Rouben Mamoulian

An Armenian born in 1898 in Tiflis, today Tbilsi, the capital of Georgia, Mamoulian spent his childhood and adolescence not only in Tiflis but Paris, Moscow, and eventually London, where he directed his first play, *The Beating at the Door*, in 1922.[13] The following year he was hired to lead the American Opera Company in Rochester, New York, where he directed numerous opera scenes and eventually full-length operas between November 1923 and July 1926. The following year he made his Broadway debut as the director of *Porgy*, a play by Dorothy and DuBose Heyward, a huge hit produced by the Theatre Guild in 1927 that ran for 367 performances. The latter venture provided indispensable training for a director of stage and film musicals, since it included four major musical set pieces.

Two years after *Porgy*, Mamoulian launched a career as a film director with *Applause*, and after directing several innovative and technologically pioneering films, including *Love Me Tonight*, Mamoulian returned to the stage in 1935 to direct *Porgy and Bess*, the operatic adaptation of *Porgy*. Following a number of successful films in the 1930s, in the 1940s he achieved his greatest popular successes as a stage director with Rodgers and Hammerstein's *Oklahoma!* (1943) and *Carousel* (1945) and other significant, if less successful, collaborations with an impressive range of composers and lyricists: George and Ira Gershwin; Jerome Kern and Oscar Hammerstein; Rodgers and Hammerstein; Vernon Duke and Howard Dietz; Harold Arlen and Johnny Mercer; Kurt Weill and Maxwell Anderson; Morton Gould and Dorothy Fields; Harry Warren and Ralph Blaine; and Cole Porter.[14] In the 1950s he was able to complete only the underrated musical film *Silk Stockings* starring Fred Astaire and Cyd Charisse, and for the last thirty years of his life Mamoulian began no major new projects. In addition to becoming increasingly selective about new work, his reputation suffered from his predilection for self-aggrandizement and for being increasingly difficult to work with. After receiving prestigious lifetime honors in his eighties, he died in squalor, his home overrun by forty pet cats. At the time of his death in 1987, Mamoulian was largely unknown to most of the general public but revered by many of his most illustrious successors.[15]

As a film director, Mamoulian remains best known for the numerous technical visual and sonic innovations he pioneered, especially in the eight films (out of sixteen total) he made between *Applause* (1929) and *The Gay*

Desperado (1936). Hugh Fordin offers a succinct summary of the technical innovations in the three films that precede *Love Me Tonight*: "the mobile camera technique" and "first two-channel sound recording" in *Applause*; the "first use of voice-over to express inner thought" in *City Streets*; and in *Dr. Jekyll and Mr. Hyde* the early scenes in which "the camera sees via the eyes of the actor," "two scenes projected simultaneously," and the "first use of nonrealistic sounds to express and underline emotional process."[16] Mamoulian biographer Mark Spergel mentions some of these techniques and adds to the list: the restoration of "the artistic use of montage and redefined close-up, split-screen, and dissolves"; "his skill at creating chiaroscuro cinematographic effect"; "the use of more than one camera for shooting a single scene"; the replacement of stock sound tracks such as generic suspense or kissing music with an imaginative use of nineteenth-century romantic orchestral and operatic classics (see table 3.1, "Borrowings"); the invention of "seamless editing"; and "the first full-length Technicolor film using its new three-color process" [in *Becky Sharp*, 1935].[17] David Luhrssen points out that the close-up of the smokestacks in the early Parisian scenes of *Love Me Tonight* "might have been the first time the zoom lens was used in place of a dolly."[18]

Mamoulian was frequently interviewed about his work, interviews in which he invariably emphasized his many technical aural and visual innovations and what he was striving to achieve artistically in his films.[19] But despite the attention drawn to so many technical firsts, a focus aided and abetted by the director himself, Mamoulian possessed a well-articulated vision of what he valued in his film and stage work (and in the arts more generally), and he spoke or wrote often about these core principles. At the heart of Mamoulian's philosophy was his decision to reject the naturalistic style of the Moscow Art Theater founded by Konstantin Stanislavski during the three to five months he studied with Evgeny Vakhtangov in 1914 in an amateur group called the Drama Studio that worked outside Stanislavski's direct purview. According to Spergel, by the time Mamoulian was involved in the Drama Studio, Vakhtangov had "drifted away from the naturalism of Stanislavsky and headed toward the approach that would bring him his greatest fame in years to come—stylization."[20] While directing *The Beating at the Door*, a production in which he adopted the reigning "naturalistic style" of Stanislavski, Mamoulian "discovered that it did not suit him" and "abandoned it for what he called 'stylization,'" the approach favored by Vakhtangov.[21]

Although Mamoulian addresses stylization in interviews over the years, his papers on "The Psychology of Sound" (a twelve-page typescript from July 1938) and his lecture on "The History of the Motion Picture," a talk he delivered at The Museum of Modern Art Film Library at Columbia University on December 6, 1939 (a sixty-page typescript), provide especially clear insights into Mamoulian's philosophy of stylization and his goals as a director.[22] For Mamoulian, "the essence of imaginative reality on the screen, is to give you the *illusion* of actuality without being actual."[23]

The basics of Mamoulian's directorial philosophy were already evident in his productions of Maurice Maeterlinck's *Sister Beatrice*, performed by the American Opera Company at Eastman Theatre in Rochester, New York, for two evenings in 1926, and his first Broadway play, *Porgy*, in 1927. Mamoulian offers a good example of sonic stylization from *Love Me Tonight* in "The Psychology of Sound" when he explains his intention behind one of the most memorable (and hysterical) stylized moments of this film, the explosion that occurs when one of Jeanette's frantic Aunts knocks over a vase upon entering the drawing-room to announce that Maurice, who has been impersonating a Baron, is nothing but a tailor. The sound of the vase hitting the floor sounds like an exploding cannon to the chateau residents in the drawing-room. By turning what should be a modest noise into an explosion, Mamoulian was not concerned with what a vase realistically *should* sound like when it hit the ground but "the *effect* of the announcement on the crowd." This is stylization at work. Mamoulian knows that the explosion comes "*at the expense* of naturalism" but chooses to disregard naturalism "because deeper than any of naturalism's precepts is the basic truth, the wildest 'deviation' justifies itself it [if] it conveys a *psychological reality*."[24]

After directing the crime film drama *City Streets* starring Gary Cooper and Sylvia Sidney, released in April 1931, in the latter months of 1931 Mamoulian completed the filming of the horror film *Dr. Jekyll and Mr. Hyde*. This last film before *Love Me Tonight*, released the first week in January 1932, starred Fredric March, who received an Academy Award as best actor for the dual role in which Jekyll was stunningly transformed, seemingly by magic, into the demonic Hyde directly on screen without the aid of cuts or other editing. About this time, as Mamoulian recalled, Adolph Zukor, the founder and president of Paramount, implored him to fill in for Lubitsch, who "was busy with other projects," and take on the direction of Chevalier and MacDonald's next film project.[25] Both of these box office stars were on munificent Paramount contracts but had been idle since their collaboration on *One Hour with You,* directed by Lubitsch and "assisted by" George Cukor.[26]

It was Cukor's demotion to assistant that led to Zukor's pleading to Mamoulian. Paramount's Head of Production B. P. "Bud" Schulberg had promised Cukor he could direct the next Chevalier–MacDonald film, but Cukor, who felt he had earned the right to be given directorial credit, disputed the diminished title and filed a lawsuit to regain directing credit of *One Hour with You.* In the end Cukor settled out of court and accepted the "assisted by" title. The good news for Cukor was that as part of the settlement he was now free to terminate his contract with Paramount and move on to a successful career at RKO starting with *What Price Hollywood?* (released in June 1932) followed by later successes with MGM.[27]

Meanwhile, Lubitsch, who was in the process of renegotiating a higher contract at Paramount, remained unavailable to direct the next Chevalier–MacDonald pairing. As Mamoulian tells the story, having lost two directors, Zukor, "with tears in his eyes," made his dramatic plea for Mamoulian to save Paramount from "the brink of bankruptcy" and direct the third Chevalier–MacDonald film.[28]

Léopold Marchand

Another strand of events leading to Mamoulian's direction of *Love Me Tonight* can be traced to October 15, 1931, when the *New York Times* announced that the French playwright Léopold Marchand had arrived in the United States, where he was hired to "prevent gaucheries from creeping into" *One Hour with You,* the second Lubitsch film to star Chevalier and MacDonald.[29] According to Mamoulian's recollections, he met Marchand at a party, which most likely occurred sometime between mid-October and the end of November:

> But I couldn't find a suitable property. And then at a party while talking to Léopold Marchand, a European writer then working at Paramount, I learned that he had a slight story idea that might be attractive. It was only two pages long, but when I read it, I thought it had a kind of fairy tale romantic magic, and I asked the studio to buy it. I then got Richard Rodgers and Lorenz Hart to develop songs for the film.[30]

In another interview Mamoulian recalled that Marchand was able to share his story "on one long sheet of yellow paper."[31] Mamoulian follows this alternative memory with a succinct encapsulation of Marchand's idea: "A tailor in Paris falls in love with a princess who lives in a château in the south of France; he arrives to collect a debt, pretending to be an aristocrat; she falls in love with him, then discovers he's a tailor, and [nevertheless] they get together."[32] Mamoulian "liked it, and started planning."[33]

Although a prolific playwright and well known as a director and actor in France, Marchand is probably best remembered as a creative collaborator with numerous writers, especially with Colette, the author of the novella *Gigi* (1944), who was also a close friend since 1919. In 1922 Marchand adapted Colette's then-recent *Chérie* (1920) for the stage and the following year Colette's earlier novel *La Vagabonde* (1910). Colette biographer Judith Thurman concluded that in their collaborations "Colette wrote most of the dialogue" while Marchand "grappled with the structure."[34]

Marchand's "slight story idea" for the future *Love Me Tonight* was actually based on a full-length play that Marchand had co-written with Paul Armont, *Le tailleur au château,* comédie en 3 actes (*The Tailor in the Castle,* a comedy in 3 acts), copyrighted on August 3, 1924.[35] A copy of the play, which is unpublished and unperformed, at least in the US, is housed in the Library of Congress, although not among the voluminous papers in the Rouben Mamoulian Collection. The alleged two-page (or perhaps one page) "slight story idea" that Marchand conveyed to Mamoulian is missing from the Rouben Mamoulian Collection, although the collection does contain an undated sixteen-page "Synopsis" and a six-page "Skeleton" dated January 8, 1932.[36] In the "Tentative Treatment" and a slightly altered Treatment that followed on January 14 and 18 respectively, followed by the "First Buff Script" (March 26) and the "First White Script" (April 19) (henceforth Buff Script and White Script), the title of the play would be abandoned in favor of the new film title, *Love Me Tonight.*[37] See table 1.1 for more information about these sources.

Richard Rodgers and Lorenz Hart

By the time Mamoulian asked Rodgers and Hart to write the songs and Rodgers to write the other instrumental music as well, the still youthful

Table 1.1 Textual Sources for *Love Me Tonight*

ORIGINAL PLAY: "*Le tailleur au château, comédie en 3 actes* de Léopold Marchand et Paul Armont." Registered for copyright on August 4, 1924, as deposit number D68502; copyright renewed on January 28, 1952 (R89463).[a] Copyright Drama Deposits, Manuscript Division, Library of Congress. Microfilm reel 1944 (Registration Numbers Between D68493 and D68502, 1924), Accession No. MS 20,849. The play entered the public domain in January 2020, after which reading and copying became permissible.

THE SYNOPSIS: "'THE TAILOR IN THE CASTLE' ('LE TAILLEUR AU CHATEAU') (Provisional Title) Synopsis of the play by LÉOPOLD MARCHAND & PAUL ARMONT" (sixteen pages in addition to a "Suggested Cast" list. Rouben Mamoulian Collection, Library of Congress, Box 78, Folder 1, Miscellany 1932. Although at sixteen pages the "Synopsis" is considerably longer than the six-page "Skeleton" that followed on January 8, 1932, based on its contents it appears to be the starting point in the process of transforming the play into a screenplay. Since Rodgers and Hart arrived in Hollywood in November 1931 under the assumption that Cukor was going to be the director of the next Chevalier–MacDonald film, it is not unreasonable to assume that the Marchand–Armont alleged "Synopsis" was drafted sometime between the songwriters' November arrival and January 7 of the new year.

THE SKELETON: "Skeleton of THE TAILOR IN THE CHATEAU." January 8, 1932. (Rouben Mamoulian Collection, Library of Congress, Box 79, Folder 4, Treatment (1) (6 pages) [THE SKELETON]

TENTATIVE TREATMENT: Rouben Mamoulian Collection, Library of Congress, Box 79, Folder 4, Treatment (2) (27 pages) "SYNOPSIS of 'LOVE ME TONIGHT'" (Tentative Treatment). January 14, 1932. This typescript includes a few minor handwritten changes.

TREATMENT: "Treatment of LOVE ME TONIGHT." January 18, 1932. (Rouben Mamoulian Collection, Library of Congress, Box 79, Folder 4, Treatment (3) (29 pages). This typescript is a slightly altered version of No. 4 that incorporates several additional handwritten changes. The two additional pages are due to a larger font.

FRENCH VERSION: "Script 1932 (1 of 4)" in French. March 9, 1932 (Sequences A and B); March 16, 1932 (Sequence C); March 17, 1932 (Sequences D and E); March 18 (Sequence F); Undated (Sequences G and H). (Rouben Mamoulian Collection, Library of Congress, Box, 78, Folder 7) [160 pages, Author's count] "DERNIER TRAITEMENT VERSION FRANÇAISE. LOVE ME TO-NIGHT. Léopold Marchand (9 Mars 1932)." The French version of the screenplay matches closely with the Buff Script (no. 7).

BUFF SCRIPT: "Script 1932 (2 of 4)." n. d. but on or about March 26, 1932. (Rouben Mamoulian Collection, Library of Congress, Box 79, Folder 1) (152 pages; 150 pages Author's count). On March 26, 1932, Jesse L. Lasky of Paramount sent to Colonel Jason S. Joy of the association of Motion Picture Producers "the first buff script" of *Love Me Tonight* and noted that the "production is scheduled to start March 28th" [the actual starting date was April 4]. Although more off-white than buff in its present state, it's possible that this screenplay version was in a more buff condition in 1932.

WHITE SCRIPT: "Script 1932 (3 of 4)." "FIRST WHITE SCRIPT." April 19, 1932. (Rouben Mamoulian Collection, Library of Congress, Box 79, Folder 2) (132 pages; 133 pages, Author's count].[b] "LOVE ME TONIGHT By Léopold Marchand and Paul Armont; Screen Play by Samuel Hoffenstein, Waldemar Young, and George Marion, Jr."

RELEASE SCRIPT: "Love Me Tonight Release Dialogue Script" (Paramount Pictures, 1932). August 15, 1932. Margaret Herrick Library 590.f-L-794. [101 pages]. Produced and directed by Rouben Mamoulian. Script by Samuel Hoffenstein, Waldemar Young, and George Marion. Lyrics by Lorenz Hart. Music by Richard Rodgers.

---

[a] Marchand died on November 25, 1952.

[b] "Script 1932 (4 of 4)," Rouben Mamoulian Collection, Library of Congress, Box 79, Folder 3, consists of a file labeled "Miscellaneous Pages."

but seasoned practitioners had been the toast of Broadway since 1925 when, after a long and increasingly dispiriting apprenticeship writing mainly amateur shows since 1919, the team became overnight sensations with the musical revue *The Garrick Gaieties* of 1925 featuring their first major song hit, "Manhattan." Over the next five years the team produced one successful, imaginative, and innovative musical after another on Broadway, including *Dearest Enemy* in 1925, *The Girl Friend* and *Peggy-Ann* in 1926, *A Connecticut Yankee* in 1927, and two hit shows for the London stage, *Lido Lady* (1926) and *Evergreen* (1930). Although these shows are rarely performed or remembered as stage works today, all of them, including the less successful runs, offered one or more memorable songs that have remained staples of the Great American Songbook (see Figure 1.2).[38]

Starting with *Dearest Enemy*, Rodgers and Hart wrote scores "that had at least some relevance to the mood, characters and situation found in a story."[39] Throughout his career with Hart and later with Hammerstein,

Figure 1.2 Richard Rodgers (right) and Lorenz Hart (left).

Rodgers also remained firm in his intention to "write scores and not isolated song numbers; therefore the particular song in question must bear a family resemblance to the other musical material in the piece."[40] Also from the beginning of their reign on Broadway, Rodgers and Hart, like Mamoulian, created shows in which "the inventions simply tumble over themselves."[41] The plots might be conventional, but Rodgers and Hart made sure that the shows contained surprising twists and offered the kind of integrated plot narratives shared by the finest contemporary American plays, goals not usually associated with American musicals before Rodgers joined Hammerstein in the 1940s.

When Mamoulian told his story of how he came to choose *The Tailor in the Castle* as his source and Rodgers and Hart to write the score, he doesn't mention what he told his friend Miles Kreuger.[42] As reported by Kreuger, Zukor wanted to again join the Viennese composer Oscar Straus with screenwriter Samson Raphaelson for *The Grand Duchess and the Waiter,* a romantic comedy Paramount had produced as a silent film in 1926.[43] Straus had successfully written the music for two previous Chevalier (and Lubitsch) vehicles, *The Smiling Lieutenant* (1931) and *One Hour with You* (1932), the latter co-starring MacDonald, and Zukor wanted to continue to capitalize on these successes. According to his recollection of the conversation with Zukor, Mamoulian "protested that I wasn't the man for the job" and suggested Lubitsch instead. Only upon learning that Lubitsch wasn't available did Mamoulian begin to warm up to the idea of directing "a light musical film" (providing he could "find a suitable property").[44] As soon as he learned about Marchand and Armont's play *The Tailor in the Castle* and decided to turn it into a musical film, he knew he wanted to ask the American composer and lyricist team Rodgers and Hart rather than a European, Straus, despite his experience and reliable track record on Broadway and in Hollywood.

At the time Mamoulian asked Rodgers and Hart to write the score for the new musical film, the pair had been going through a period of transition from Broadway to Hollywood. Earlier in 1931, the team completed a satire of Hollywood, *America's Sweetheart*, which had a brief Broadway run between February and June 1931 (135 performances). After a continuous stream of mostly successful as well as innovative stage shows on Broadway starting in 1925, *Sweetheart* would be their last for four years.[45] Their first Hollywood project consisted of three songs for *The Hot Heiress*, released in March 1931. In November they returned to Los Angeles to begin work on a new and more ambitious film musical, which they were told would be directed by Cukor. Without knowing that Cukor was leaving Paramount, and unaware of Mamoulian's experience and skill as a director for the musical stage, including numerous operas and operettas, Rodgers and Hart were initially disappointed as well as surprised to learn that Mamoulian was assigned to direct the new Chevalier film. As he explains in *Musical Stages*, Rodgers was concerned that "such melodramatic offerings as *Applause* and *Dr. Jekyll and Mr. Hyde*" did not bode well for the "deft, delicate touch" needed to do justice to a Chevalier vehicle.[46]

After meeting the "owlish" and "exuberant" Mamoulian, Rodgers quickly became convinced "that there could be no better director for *Love Me Tonight*,"[47] and on December 1, 1931, *Variety* announced that the lyricist and composer team were "to get to work on the words and music immediately."[48] As Studio Relations Committee (the forerunner of the Production Code Administration) files reveal, by January 11, 1932, Paramount had sent Hart's finished lyrics for "Isn't It Romantic?" to the censors for review.[49] This was three days after the date on the Skeleton. On January 22, four days after the date of the altered Treatment, Hart's lyrics to "The Song of Paree" would follow.[50]

During the planning stages of *Love Me Tonight* Mamoulian also asked Rodgers to do something that the composer had not previously imagined possible. This important passage merits a leisurely quotation:

Owlish, with a thick crop of black hair and an exuberant manner, Mamoulian had a concept of filming that was almost exactly what we had in mind. Like us, he was convinced that a musical film should be created in musical terms—that dialogue, song and scoring should all be integrated as closely as possible so that the final product would have a unity of style and design. Fortunately, he was the producer as well as director of the film and had complete autonomy. One of the first things he insisted on was that I compose all the background music, not simply the music for the songs. This was—and still is—highly unusual, since film scoring has generally been left to composers specializing in the field. It is more or less stop-watch composing, with the writer creating musical themes to fit precisely into a prescribed number of frames. I had no background in this sort of work but I found it extremely challenging and fun to do, and it certainly helped in giving the film the desired creative unity.[51]

Rodgers leaves out Mamoulian's emphasis on the crucial importance of the songs themselves. This is how the director explained his intentions forty years after he asked Paramount to purchase Marchand's "slight story idea":

> I then got Richard Rodgers and Lorenz Hart to develop the songs for the film. You understand, all the songs were carefully planned, with the lyrics to advance the story line, and their place in the story itself designed before the writers of the screenplay were engaged. This is the way an original musical film should be developed, in my opinion, but it also seldom happens like this. When the screenwriters—Hoffenstein, Marion Jr., and Young—came on the picture it was their job to construct the scenes and bridge the dialogue between the song numbers, so that the songs flowed from the action sequences and the actors didn't stop and sing a song. It worked perfectly.[52]

The Genesis and Writing of the Screenplay

The rest of this chapter will focus on how the main textual sources (the Synopsis, Skeleton, Treatment, and two screenplays--the Buff Script and the White Script) combined and evolved to transform a fairy tale play into a fairy tale film musical. Table 1.1 identifies the main textual sources from January to April 1932, all but the Synopsis precisely dated.[53] Since it is unrealistic in a short book such as this one to treat all these sources comprehensively, the chapter will highlight three areas of particular significance and interest: 1) the initial musical connection between Maurice the tailor and Jeanette the princess; 2) the revelation of Maurice's lowly status and the end of the tale; and 3) the introduction of the songs leading to their final placement in the film. For a Plot Summary of the film as released readers are referred to the back matter of this volume.

1) *The initial musical connection between Maurice the tailor and Jeanette the princess*

One of the most discussed and widely praised portions of *Love Me Tonight* is the marvelous cinematic and musical imagination displayed in the complex montage of the song "Isn't It Romantic?" that Jane Feuer called a "passed-along song."[54] In his "History of the Motion Picture" Mamoulian recalls that what he describes as a "traveling song" was inspired by a fairy tale his grand-mother told him when he was a child:

> She used to tell me fairytales, and one of the charming ones I remember was about a princess who was making a piece of embroidery. A gust of wind snatched it away from her and carried it across many lands and many waters, landing it finally into the lap of a young and handsome prince. He at once fell in love with her who made that embroidery and decided to find her and marry her. So he travelled over the face of the earth until he found his prin-cess. I thought it a lovely idea, and used it, with slight variations, of course.[55]

Strikingly, the sixteen-page (double-spaced) freely adapted Synopsis based on Marchand and Armont's *Le tailleur au château* does not include any reference to this remarkable passed-along/traveling song (or any other songs). Instead, we simply meet Maurice Hortigan (listed as Chevalier in the "Suggested Cast") in his tailor's shop (1) and then meet the eighteen-year-old princess Nady de Pontbrisson (sixteen in the play) at her chateau (listed as Jeanette McDonald [*sic*] in the "Suggested Cast") (3). When Mamoulian drafted the six-page (single-spaced) Skeleton on January 8, 1932, however, it not only included "Isn't It Romantic?" but several other songs. The basic ap-proach of "Isn't It Romantic?" in the Skeleton also closely parallels its treatment in the film, although it takes place later in the story when Maurice himself, rather than just his song, has left the shop to travel to the chateau to confront the Viscount Ruggles and collect the unpaid money owed for his many suits.[56]

The Treatment dated January 14 (slightly modified on January 18) retains both the placement and the context of "Isn't It Romantic?" described in the Skeleton. Prospective viewers now can follow the travels of the song, al-though in both Treatments the delayed appearance of the song doesn't allow time for the profound connection between the tailor and the princess to take root. The Buff Script (March 26) will attempt to remedy this dramatic infe-licity when Maurice's journey to the chateau *follows* the travels of his song that has already begun to cast its magic musical spell on his future princess.

2) The revelation of Maurice's lowly status and how the fairy tale ends

The revelation that Maurice is "nothing but a tailor" forms the belatedly climactic moment in the original play and in all the screenplay drafts from

January on.[57] This section will show how the crucial revelation evolved and, more significantly, how Jeanette responded to the unwelcome news that Maurice, who had been impersonating a Baron, is in reality a member of the working class, what the Duke dismisses as a tradesman.

In the January sources (Synopsis, Skeleton, and Treatment), the revelation comes from the mouths of babes, along with some prodding from the Baron de la Huttelière, the character who eventually becomes the Count de Savignac. In the Synopsis the jealous and suspicious Baron notices that Kiki (Maurice's child assistant, about ten, who does not appear in the play) has approached Maurice, who pretends not to know the boy. The Baron then questions Kiki, who reveals Maurice's identity. The Baron threatens Maurice with exposure, after which Maurice leaves the chateau immediately taking Kiki with him, leaving Nady wondering where Maurice has gone, and why. After Maurice and Kiki return to the Parisian shop, Gilbert (listed as Ruggles in the Synopsis's "Suggested Cast") figures out a way to purchase orders from Maurice's shop surreptitiously.

In a plot point traceable to the Marchand–Armont play, it is not until Nady arrives with the Duke and Duchess to purchase clothing from his Parisian shop that Maurice Adolphe Hortigan in the play) reveals his profession and lower social station. In the play, audiences also learn in the final moments at the tailor's shop that centuries earlier the first Baron Hortigan served as the tailor to King Louis X le Hutin (Louis X the Quarrelsome, who reigned from 1314 to 1316), and that, unknown to the present-day Hortigan, had retained his noble status and was thus worthy to wed Nady. The Synopsis retains the delayed revelation, which is analogous to a deus ex machina.[58] As a way of appreciating Maurice for listening to his "interminable stories when no one else would" (16), the elderly and wealthy Count de Morneplaine solves the problem of Maurice's lowly social and financial position by adopting the tailor and bequeathing to him his own title and fortune. In future treatments and screenplay drafts, Morneplaine, along with the Duchess, will vanish without a trace.

In the Skeleton, another child, this time a slightly older girl named Mitzi who has replaced Kiki, naïvely reveals the nature of Maurice's profession to Roland Young.[59] Young hurries off to share the revelation to the Duke, who passes the news on to everyone, except for Jeanette, that "the-son-of-a gun is nothing but a tailor."[60] As in the Synopsis, Jeanette realizes in the Skeleton she loves Maurice no matter why he has abruptly left the chateau and is the last to learn his professional identity, although in the Skeleton she doesn't have to visit Maurice's shop in Paris to find out what happened. The Skeleton also introduces a key event in the plot that will be retained with various modifications throughout the next four months and forms the dramatic conclusion of the film: Jeanette riding her horse and catching up with Maurice, who has taken the train to Paris.

The Treatment offers a few noteworthy new plot points. Instead of Jeanette joining Maurice on the train, the lovebirds get off the train after Maurice has shouted out his humble origins and a vegetable cart comes by and offers to take them to Paris. Meanwhile, Mitzi (renamed Madeleine), while waiting for Maurice to return to the chateau, has a conversation with the Duke in which she praises Maurice's character and notices the family crest hanging from the wall. She asks the Duke how he can be so sure there are no tailors hidden among his noble ancestors. The camera takes this as a cue for a close-up of a needle and thread. This revelation jogs the Duke's memory and causes him to recollect that the ancestor who built the ancient chateau was also a "son-of-a-gun," who, as in the play, happened to serve as the tailor to the fourteenth-century French king Charles V.[61] Mamoulian explains: "I won't go into the details of this scene now; it has to be worked out, but at the conclusion of it we see the Duke pacified and convinced by Madeleine and willing to accompany her to Paris" (29).

The Buff and White scripts written by Hoffenstein, Young, and Marion have Maurice himself (not Kiki, Mitzi, or Madeleine) ultimately reveal his profession and class to Jeanette. What prompts the question in each case is Maurice's expertise in fitting Jeanette's riding-habit. In the Buff Script Jeanette simply asks, "Who are you?," and Maurice responds, "I'm a tailor" (G-98–99); in the White Script and final film she confronts Maurice with the observation that the riding-habit is "too perfect" (F-10).

The details of Jeanette's reaction to this shocking revelation differ, but in all the screenplays Jeanette needs time for betrayal and anger to metamorphose into acceptance and love. In the Buff Script she gives Maurice an hour to leave the chateau. In contrast to the Synopsis, Skeleton, and Treatment, however, Maurice is in no hurry to leave, despite a confrontation in which Jeanette expresses with sudden anger, "I despise you" (H-18). In another new Buff Script variation Valentine is delighted to learn that Maurice is a tailor and proceeds to seriously flirt with him. That night, the devilish Maurice deliberately drops a flowerpot which awakens both Valentine and Jeanette.[62]

The appearance of Maurice seemingly leaving Valentine's bedroom leads to yet another angry scene between Jeanette and Maurice. The distraught Jeanette wakes up the rest of the chateau and Maurice reveals his profession to the Duke, who launches the passed-along (or traveling) song "The Son-of-a-Gun Is Nothing but a Tailor." The remaining plot of the Buff Script follows the final version relatively closely, but unlike any of the other versions the scoring directions indicate additional reprises of "And a Woman Needs Something Like That" and "The Man for Me."

In the White and Release Scripts Jeanette realizes the truth of her pledge to Maurice that accompanies "Love Me Tonight" ("Whoever you are— whatever you are—wherever you are—I love you").[63] After the tailor and his princess are reunited, the final words of the film are delivered by the three Aunts who have now completed the tapestry they have been sewing throughout the film. The tapestry depicts, as it turns out erroneously, a prince on a horse saving a princess: "Once upon a time there was a Princess and a Prince Charming. Who was not a Prince. But who was charming. And they lived happily ever after...."[64]

Despite the Aunts' plot reversal in the image they have sewn on the tapestry that viewers see completed at the end of the film, it would be a challenge to come up with another film ending that so successfully demonstrates the essence of a fairy tale or a fairy tale film musical. Although there are some departures between *Love Me Tonight* and various recurring tropes inherent in the typical fairy tale film musical, the Aunts' encapsulation of the story at the end of the film (concluding with their pronouncement "and they lived happily ever after"), clearly captures the spirit as well as the letter of the fairy tale genre. Rick Altman's seminal analysis fits in well with Mamoulian's stylized approach to story-telling: "In the *fairy tale musical* (so named because of its tendency to predicate the future of a kingdom on the romance of a 'princess' and her suitor), the creation of an imaginary kingdom creates ample opportunity to stress the transcendence of the real that characterizes the musical as a whole in comparison to other Hollywood genres."[65] In other words, the creation of an imaginary kingdom such as the world of Princess Jeanette's chateau enhances the fairy tale musical film's capacity to transcend the constraints of the "real world" and differentiates its intentions and purposes from the other film musical genres explored by Altman, the "folk" musical (*Oklahoma!*) and the "back stage" musical (*42nd Street*).

3) *The introduction of songs and their placement in the film*

The Skeleton names only three songs by name heard in the finished film: 1) "How Are You?" (eventually called "Song of Paris" in the Buff and White Scripts); 2) "Isn't It Romantic?"; and 3) "The Son-of-a-Gun Is Nothing but a Tailor." This trio of songs, the first two and last songs in the film, serve as bookends for the songs in between that at this point in the process remained unidentified. The Skeleton also mentions a "work song" that will evolve into the memorable rhythmic rhapsody known as the "Symphony of Noises" at the outset of the film and another untitled song set in the chateau's riding stables later in the film, a "tender scene" between Jeanette, Maurice, and Jeanette's horse.[66] In the White Script this unnamed song will be imaginatively transformed into Jeanette's "Lover." The Skeleton also describes a song called "It's Only Eighty Rooms, but It's a Home" and a "Sailor's Song" that Maurice sings to the chateau residents, both of which will eventually be discarded.

The Treatment introduces only one new song by name that will appear in the final film: the title song "Love Me Tonight." In a striking departure from the final version, however, it is sung by Valentine, not by the central lovers Maurice and Jeanette.[67] In addition to the retention of "It's Only Eighty Rooms, but It's a Home" (now clearly designated for the Duke and his family), the Treatment includes several songs designed for specific situations that will evaporate in the Buff Script in March. These include an untitled song between Maurice and Jeanette described as a comedy song to accompany their meeting over the game of solitaire, a solo song for Maurice called "What Could I Do?" when he finds himself alone in the Louis the Fourteenth Room directly after "It's Only Eighty Rooms," and a humorous song that addresses Maurice's limited table etiquette to accompany a "short dinner scene from soup to black coffee" ("I Find This Much Simpler and Nicer").

The Treatment includes more items of interest: 1) it suggests the possibility that Chevalier might sing one or two unnamed specialty "Chevalier-type" songs after dinner (a song perhaps like the "Sailor's Song" in the Skeleton); 2) it returns to the song idea in the stables that will eventually become "Lover"; 3) it describes an untitled love song shared by Maurice and Jeanette separated at a distance on a sleepless night that matches the scene directions included with the unpublished lyrics of "Give Me Just a Moment"; and finally, 4) for the first time, it describes incidental music to accompany

the climactic scene in which Jeanette and her horse chase down and eventually stops Maurice's moving train with inter-cutting between a horse theme
and a train theme.[68]

With the exception of "Lover," the Buff Script completes the introduction
of previously missing film songs, "A Woman Needs Something Like That,"
"The Poor Apache," and "Mimi," although the context of the latter will not be
determined until the White Script. The Buff Script also introduces a "Letter
Song," later renamed "The Man for Me," that was removed from the fin-
ished film. The idea of an untitled "It's Only Eighty Rooms" remains, and the
Buff Script retains the title as well as the instructions to sing "What Could
I Do?" The Buff Script also introduces an untitled "song by the domestics"
preceding "A Woman Needs Something Like That" that will be dropped
from the White Script. Curiously, the love song set in the stables in the
Skeleton and Treatment disappears in the Buff Script, but in the White Script
Mamoulian and his screenwriters found a way to use this temporarily abandoned love song designated for Jeanette and Maurice in the stables addressed
to a horse. The solution was to write a love song for Jeanette to sing to her
horse (overheard by Maurice) before Jeanette's horse, carriage, and pas-
senger tumble into a ditch in front of her future partner. In addition to its
intrinsic cleverness, the idea of a suggestive surrogate love song directed to
a horse rather than to a man likely went a long way toward getting its lyrics
past the censors at the Studio Relations Committee.[69]

The late decision to have Maurice and Jeanette meet in the countryside
allowed the future lovers an opportunity to demonstrate the kind of resistance that would soon mark the Fred Astaire and Ginger Rogers films starting
with *The Gay Divorcee* in 1934. Such antagonism masks the attraction between the romantic couples and prolongs their eventual coupling, major
components of the fairy tale musical. It is a trope well baked into the genre as
Altman states succinctly in his seminal analysis of the fairy tale musical: "The
refusal of the prospective partner to fall immediately prey remains a necessary plot device."[70]

Some of the material that made it from the White Script to the Release
Script in August contained material that the Production Code Administration
insisted on removing when the film was rereleased more than a decade later.
These passages will be discussed in chapter 4. Presumably in the interest of
keeping the film within the approximately 90- to 100-minute normal film
lengths of the period rather than potential problems with censorship, various lines from the White Script were never filmed. In the vast majority of

these omissions, the present writer concurs with the wisdom of Mamoulian and his trio of screenwriters. A rare exception is this chapter's epigraph, a memorable exchange between Gilbert and Valentine that was regrettably removed prior to the final shooting.

Aside from this small misdemeanor, Mamoulian's hard work in the Synopsis, Skeleton, and Treatment, and the inspired screenplays of Hoffenstein, Young, and Marion, paid off with rich and lasting dividends. Nearly a century later viewers might share the opinion espoused by Lamar Trotti, who represented the Studio Relations Committee, to Jesse L Lasky of Paramount one day after reading the April 19 White Script: "May I add that in general this is one of the most delightful scripts I have ever read."[71]

2

Songs by Rodgers and Hart

"In the face of the pin-wheel brilliance of some of Larry's work, one is inclined to forget the deeper phases of his writing."

Richard Rodgers on Lorenz Hart (1951)

"He writes music to depict story and character and is, therefore, himself a dramatist. . . . He composes in order to make words fly higher or cut deeper than they would without the aid of his music."

Oscar Hammerstein 2nd on Richard Rodgers (1951)

Introduction

On June 11, 1933, nine months after the release of *Love Me Tonight* the previous August, Richard Rodgers boasted in a letter to his wife, Dorothy, about the success of one of his songs: " 'Lover' is one of the six best sellers in the country, you'll be glad to know."[1] Eventually, "Lover," the first of a long series of famous Rodgers waltzes, would be listed in the "Hit Parade of a Half Century" and "*Variety's* Golden 100 Tin Pan Alley."[2] Twenty years after *Love Me Tonight,* with new lyrics and an even newer musical treatment, it acquired new popularity, notoriety, and initially Rodgers's wrath (later retracted), with Peggy Lee's frenzied Latin version arranged by Gordon Jenkins.[3] According to Don Tyler's *Hit Songs 1900–1955,* "Lover" "became one of the most recorded songs of the pre-rock era."[4]

Ever since it was "passed along" from Maurice Chevalier's Parisian tailor shop to Jeanette MacDonald's country chateau, another song from *Love Me Tonight,* "Isn't It Romantic?" has imprinted itself even more indelibly in the Great American Songbook and in popular culture in general, including future films and even perfume ads. Preston Sturges featured the song prominently in the romantic comedy *The Lady Eve* (1941) starring Barbara Stanwyck and Henry Fonda and reprised the following year in Sturges's *The*

Love Me Tonight. Geoffrey Block, Oxford University Press. © Oxford University Press 2024.
DOI: 10.1093/9780197566220.003.0002

Palm Beach Story. Billy Wilder used the song in no fewer than three films, *The Major and the Minor* (1942), *A Foreign Affair* (1948), and most famously in Audrey Hepburn's early film success *Sabrina* (1954), in which the uniden- tified song plays a memorable role in driving the plot at strategic romantic moments in the story.[5] It also naturally appeared in the film *Isn't It Romantic* (1948).[6]

Fifty years later, "Isn't It Romantic?" gained distinction as the earliest song to make the list of 100 songs in American Film Institute's *100 Years… 100 Songs* at #73, the only Rodgers and Hart song to attain this distinction.[7] While Alec Wilder in his classic survey *American Popular Song* briefly discussed "Lover" and "Mimi," he devoted nearly two pages to "Isn't It Romantic?," which he lauded as "a perfect song" with a "very beautiful verse," and a "beautifully executed" climax on the word "love."[8] But as with the film itself, the legacy of "Isn't It Romantic?" far surpassed its popularity in its own time. It may have been *Love Me Tonight*'s most popular song with 37,266 copies sold, but this sales figure places the future iconic song as the second *lowest* song among the top-selling dozen songs introduced in Paramount film musicals between 1929 and 1933.[9] The verdict of history offers an alternative narrative. While the other songs on Paramount's early hit parade have long vanished from our memories, "Isn't It Romantic?" remains familiar to millions who have not even heard of the film in which it made its debut.

"Lover" and "Isn't It Romantic?" were the major hits, but three others among the eight songs in *Love Me Tonight* were published when the movie came out ("Mimi," "The Poor Apache," and the title song). "Lover," "Isn't it Romantic?," and "Mimi" were published in the first *Rodgers and Hart Song Book* (1951), and "Love Me Tonight" joined this trio in a new R&H an- thology published in 1995.[10] With the possible exception of the title song, the lyrics to "Lover" and "Isn't It Romantic?" are so closely linked to specific and topical dramatic situations (e.g., a princess singing a love song to her horse) that it seemed necessary to substitute new, more generic lyrics.

Although not all the songs come across as "tunes," *Love Me Tonight*'s grand total of eight songs is greater than what viewers will see and hear in the Fred Astaire and Ginger Rogers films that will soon follow. *Follow the Fleet* comes close to this number with seven songs. Most of the rest have five or six, but *Carefree* has only four. About half of the songs in *Love Me Tonight* are di- egetic, a term appropriated (or misappropriated) from the ancient Greeks. By scholarly consensus reached in the past fifty years or so a diegetic song has come to mean a stage song or a film song in which the characters know they are singing.[11] A prime example is *Cabaret* in which the 1966 stage version directed by Hal Prince contained a mixture of diegetic and nondiegetic songs, while the 1972 film version directed by Bob Fosse scrapped the nondiegetic songs and retained (or added) only diegetic songs sung at the Kit Kat Klub (or in one instance at a beer garden).

The diegetic songs in *Love Me Tonight* include "Isn't It Romantic?" (both the original version and its reprise), "Lover," "Mimi" (original version and reprise), and "The Poor Apache." The only published song that was not presented diegetically in the film was the central love duet "Love Me Tonight." With "Isn't It Romantic?" it may be difficult to discern from the verse and first chorus whether Maurice is aware he is singing, but when Emile joins with the words "a very catchy strain," all doubt is removed. As the song gets passed along, it becomes clear that the composer in the taxi and then on the train knows he is copying down Maurice's songs (he even identifies the pitches as he does so) and the soldiers know they are listening to this song. One soldier complains that it is "too damn long." The Gypsy violinist also knows he is playing Maurice's tune, although he doesn't know who wrote it. From the context it's also clear that when the taxi driver sings "da, da, da, da, da" and then whistles "da, da, da, da, da, da" he is conscious of his actions, and when Jeanette stands on her balcony, she knows she is hearing Maurice's song, which she describes as "a dream that can be *heard*" [italics mine].

With "Lover" we know that Jeanette is singing a song to her horse, and viewers can see that Maurice hears her doing this, which he confirms in the subsequent dialogue, when he asks Jeanette whether he can sing the song "Mimi" to her. After all, didn't she just sing "Lover" to him? It's a little mysterious how the next morning the Duke, Gilbert, the Aunts, and the Count all seem to know "Mimi," but they can't get Maurice's serenade to Jeanette out of their heads. Finally, Maurice prefaces his diegetic song "The Poor Apache" by informing the chateau residents at the post-hunt ball, "I'll tell you the story of one [Apache] that I have known."

Three of the diegetic songs ("Isn't It Romantic?," "Lover," and the reprise of "Mimi") and three of the nondiegetic songs ("The Song of Paree," "A Woman Needs Something Like That," and "The Son-of-a-Gun Is Nothing but a Tailor") might be also characterized as integrated songs, thus "setting the stage" (or in this case the film studio) for the conscious furtherance of integration a decade in the future when Mamoulian and Rodgers joined with Hammerstein to create *Oklahoma!* Broadway historian Mark N. Grant contends that *Love Me Tonight* was "arguably the first completely integrated musical comedy on stage or screen."[12]

In fact, the principles of integration can be traced earlier to nineteenth-century European operetta and the American musicals of Jerome Kern, P. G. Wodehouse, and Guy Bolton and their so-called Princess Theatre and comparable musicals that regularly appeared at that theater in New York City between 1915 and 1919.[13] In an interview from 1917 Kern expressed two of the essential principles of integration that came to be attributed to *Oklahoma!* The first is "that the musical numbers should carry on the action of the play" and the second is that these numbers "should be representative of the personalities of the characters who sing them."[14]

Oscar Hammerstein would restate Kern's two principles and add a few more, in particular that songs should flow directly from the dialogue, that dances should advance the plot and enhance the dramatic meaning of the songs that precede them, and that the orchestra, through accompaniment and underscoring, should also parallel, complement, or advance the plot. Including Kern's conviction that songs should advance the plot and should express the characters who sing them, *Love Me Tonight* for the most part follows four of the five principles espoused by Kern and Hammerstein.[15] The fifth relates to dance, not a major element in this musical.

Dance historian John Mueller was perhaps first to argue that dance has also served to advance integration in film nearly a decade before *Oklahoma!* He marks this milestone with Fred Astaire's dance sequence to the music of Cole Porter's "Night and Day" in the film *The Gay Divorcee* (1934), which Mueller contends constitutes "the first of Astaire's major plot-advancing numbers in film."[16] Dance doesn't advance the plot in *Love Me Tonight*. Aside from a short ballroom dance after the hunt, it plays no role at all.

The remaining portion of this chapter will introduce the eight songs in *Love Me Tonight* that include lyrics and their reprises. The instrumental numbers, leitmotivs, underscoring, and musical borrowings will be discussed in chapter 3. In the discussion of each song the focus will be on the dramatic contexts, what's going in the lyrics and music, how story, words, and music work together either diegetically or nondiegetically, and the extent to which they are integrated into the fabric of the film.

The principal manuscript sources used in the discussion that follows are the dated Conductor's Scores that directly preceded the film score. They are currently held at the Paramount Archives.[17] Notated in piano reduction with lyrics (when applicable), they closely follow Rodgers's undated holograph vocal scores located in the Library of Congress and the New York Public Library. Unlike Rodgers's vocal scores, the Conductor's Scores also include various notations for instrumentation to be performed either by orchestral families (woodwinds, strings, "brass muted," etc.) or identified by a particular instrument. The Conductor's Scores were orchestrated by John Leipold (1888–1970), perhaps after some discussion with Rodgers.

THE SONGS

"The Song of Paree" (4:43–7:26)

Conductor's Score, January 21, 1932. Hart's lyrics sent to the Studio Relations Committee (the forerunner of the Production Code Administration) on January 22.

"The Song of Paree" opens with the same whole-tone melody heard nearly unceasingly throughout the previous instrumental cue number. We will call this melody the "Street Scene Tune" (see Musical Example 2.1).

The whole-tone scale was so closely associated with the French composer Claude Debussy that even fourteen years after his death its ubiquitous presence in the "Street Scene Tune" as a playful instrumental refrain between the sung portions of "The Song of Paree" helps create the sense of a French urban atmosphere. The horns heard in various places in both the "Street Scene" and "The Song of Paree" evoke Gershwin's more contemporary *An American in Paris* (1927) with its authentic French taxi horns referred to as klaxons (to rhyme with "Anglo Saxons") in the main chorus of the soon-to-arrive "Song of Paree."

In Rodgers's holograph vocal scores in the Library of Congress and New York Public Library and Paramount's Conductor's Score, the song opens with Maurice singing the phrase "Lovely morning Song of Paree, you are much too loud for me" on a single pitch (E). In the film he speaks the line, the first of numerous places in the film where a character speaks the rhythm of the lyrics instead of singing the pitches indicated by Rodgers. Rhythmic

Musical Example 2.1 "Street Scene Tune"

speech is most prevalent in "A Woman Needs Something Like That," in which Dr. Pontignac doesn't sing *any* of the pitches Rodgers wrote for him and even Jeanette mostly speaks the rhythms of the score (though in contrast to the Doctor, Jeanette does sing when the score asks her to). The discussion that follows for "The Song of Paree" and future songs will take a moment to mention most of Rodgers's intended melodic passages that were converted to rhythmic speech. In this case Maurice quickly moves from speech to song, beginning with "It's not a Sonata by Mozart."[18]

Interestingly, the section labeled "chorus" that follows a slightly longer version of the "Street Scene Tune" is not sung by Maurice or by his friends and shopkeepers until toward the end of the song. In fact, although pitches are clearly marked, a grand total of four words of the chorus are sung, all on half notes to the words "How's your bakery?" The virtually unsung performance of written pitches creates a highly unusual form in which a "talky" (half-sung) verse is followed by a mostly spoken chorus. Paradoxically, what listeners of a song almost invariably perceive as the main tune of a song in "The Song of Paree" presents the characteristics found more commonly in a less melodic introductory verse. The tune of the chorus *is* present, however, in the *orchestra* underneath the rhythmic and usually rhymed dialogue; but since the vocalized speech overshadows the accompaniment, it can be difficult to hear.[19]

Immediately after Maurice's final greeting "how are you?" addressed to the Jewish store owner Monsieur Cohen, Maurice enters his shop, and the orchestra now allows listeners to clearly hear what the chorus would have sounded like had they had a chance to hear it sung. The "How Are You Interlude" accompanies Maurice's activities in the shop, such as taking off his coat or dusting (actions indicated in specific musical moments in the Conductor's Score). The Interlude, an unsung highlight to the score added late in the production by Leipold on July 15 after the film had been shot, is jazzy and syncopated in a manner that resembles the Charleston.[20] It will return to accompany Maurice's carefully synchronized movements when he arrives at the chateau and begins to explore its cavernous interior (discussed in chapter 3).

The nondiegetic "Song of Paree" is part of the action it advances. The action itself is simple and occurs in real time, starting from when Maurice shouts out his window complaining about the "Symphony of Noises" and continuing until he reaches his shop and shuts the door three minutes later. Viewers get a good sense of Maurice the tailor during his journey. The verse, which in retrospect turns out to be the song's chorus, is a song extolling the virtues of Paris and all it has to offer compared to other cities in the world, a city so wonderful that a person "would sell your wife and daughter for just one Latin Quarter."

The part of the song labeled chorus consists of a series of conversations with shop keepers and other people Maurice knows, some on the street and some in their open windows. It's clear that Maurice is a man about town with the ladies but that he's also in debt with the grocer. When he asks one young woman if she's free on Friday, a second woman interrupts with irritation that Friday is *her* day. After his exchange with the grocer, Maurice sees a third woman, with whom he has seemingly had a relationship, walking with another man. When Maurice asks his "coy friend" if she now has "some other boyfriend," the man explains that she is his wife. The final person Maurice greets is the Jewish store owner Monsieur Cohen, whose otherness is depicted not only by his dress and Yiddish accent but as the sole person who speaks French (other than "Bonjour") when he greets Maurice with "Comment ça va?" Interestingly, this final exchange does not appear in Rodgers's handwritten score, but it can be found in all the other manuscripts, including the lyric sheets and the Conductor's Score. Unfortunately, all of these sources identify Monsieur Cohen as a "kike," the most common ethnic slur used against Jews at the time and continuing to the present day.

"Isn't It Romantic?" (11:52–17:32)

Conductor's Score, May 11, 1932; Hart's lyrics sent to the Studio Relations Committee on January 11.

"Isn't It Romantic?" is the only song from *Love Me Tonight* in which a portion is known to have been drafted for an earlier musical. The earlier song, "Now I Believe," was deleted prior to the out-of-town tryouts for *America's Sweetheart*, which opened on Broadway on February 10, 1931. In his introductory note to "Now I Believe" in the first edition of *The Complete Lyrics of Lorenz Hart*, Robert Kimball stated that "the music for the refrain [i.e., chorus] does not survive, but the music for the verse became music for the verse of 'Isn't It Romantic?'"[21] Although Rodgers's draft contains no lyrics, it is easy to determine that the lyrics and music fit as perfectly for the chorus of "Isn't It Romantic?" as they did for the verse of "Now I Believe." When record producer Ben Bagley found out the chorus of "Now I Believe" had been

located, he recorded both the verse and the chorus of the song in 1993.[22]
Bagley's recording offers a logical and persuasive alignment of Rodgers's
score and Hart's lyrics.

Like "The Song of Paree," "Isn't It Romantic?" is thoroughly integrated
into the dramatic narrative, in which viewers can trace the journey of a
melody from Maurice's tailor shop all the way to Princess Jeanette's chateau.
The partially rhymed dialogue between Maurice and his admiring customer
Émile (book/look and thread/wed) precedes Maurice's singing of the verse
and chorus. Until this point the song is integrated but not diegetic, but by
the time Émile acknowledges that Maurice has sung "a very catchy strain,"
the song has switched gears to the diegetic mode. From then on the song
will continue diegetically as the song gets passed along from a taxi driver
to a composer who sings the pitches of the song in the cab and on the train.
Soldiers on the train hear the composer singing Maurice's song, and soon
we see them singing the "catchy strain" as a chorus on their march in the
country. A young Gypsy violinist hears the soldiers and plays the song at his
camp, where the romantic strains of Maurice's song waft over Jeanette's balcony. Rodgers and Hart's song and Mamoulian's imaginative film montage
have now linked the future lovers, and viewers know that the answer posed
by the song's title is "yes."

As with "It's Got to Be Love" from *On Your Toes* four years later, Rodgers in
"Isn't It Romantic?" organized the conventional 32-bar song form into two
16-bar phrases (A A') rather than the more frequently employed four 8-bar
phrases organized as A-A-B-A.[23] The final four bars of the first A are unique.
The parallel measures of the second A return to the opening phrase at their
conclusion, but with a small albeit significant change in the lyrics at the end
of the song from "Isn't it romantic?" to "isn't it romance?"

A	a 8	"Isn't it romantic?"
	b 8	"I hear the breezes playing"
A'	A 8	"Isn't it romantic?"
	b 4	"Sweet symbols in the moonlight"
	a' 4	"In love perchance? Isn't it romance?"

The musical phrase associated with the title begins with an upbeat before its downbeat on "-man-tic" after which the phrase repeats to the words
"music in the night," now on the downbeat of the second full measure of the
song. A striking characteristic of the opening phrase is its sense of resolution

in that the question "isn't it romantic?" provides its own answer. If Rodgers didn't have so much in store for the next thirty measures, it would be possible to end the song right then. The slightly altered musical question "isn't it romance?" returns to bring the song to a close. Although Rodgers was familiar with a considerable amount of classical music (as we will see in the classical borrowing noted in chapter 3), it is highly unlikely that Rodgers was thinking of Franz Joseph Haydn or Ludwig van Beethoven. But since great minds can think alike, Rodgers has clearly come up with the same idea his classical predecessors used in a string quartet and symphony, respectively: a song which begins at its end and ends at its beginning (see Musical Example 2.2a–f).

With the exception of the surprising final and highest note of the first "A," the D-flat that gets the last "word," the two halves of the first "A" are the same. This means we have heard the first five notes of the song (starting with the five syllables it takes to sing "Isn't It Romantic?") four times in the first eight measures, twice beginning on the upbeat and twice on the downbeat. The D-flat that ends the first half of A (on "word") descends a half step to a whole note on C to begin with the "b" phrase of A, which consists of two 4-bar phrases that are identical until their final note. What follows is an even more surprising downward leap from a C to a D-flat on the word "love," now resolving up a half step to begin the second A section.

After the first eight bars of the second A ("a") and the first two bars of its "b" segment brings the song back to where we were at this point in the first A section, Rodgers takes an E-flat up to C in the space between the syllable "-bove" and the word "while" (mm. 12–13). When he returns to this passage in bars 27–28, he alters it by adding a G on the way up to C (i.e., E-flat–G–C–E-flat instead of E-flat–C). The altered rising melody sets up the apex note F fittingly on the word "love." Also unifying the melody is a dotted quarter eighth-note rhythm in bars 27–28 ("Do you mean that I will fall in" ending before the climactic F on "love"). After "love perchance?" the chorus concludes with a return to the opening of the "a" rhythm that has been heard in both the "a" and "b" passages of the song (mm. 3, 7, 11, 15, 19, and 25), but one syllable shorter to accommodate the change from "romantic" to "romance."

These details reveal a song of extraordinary melodic and rhythmic unity, economy, and subtlety. Before Hart wrote his lyrics Rodgers only had a title

Musical Example 2.2a-f Beginnings and Endings

a."Isn't It Romantic?" (beginning, mm. 1–2)

b."Isn't It Romantic?" (conclusion, mm. 30–32)

c. Haydn: String Quartet in G Major, Op. 33, No. 5, first movement (beginning, mm. 1–2)

d. Haydn: String Quartet in G Major, Op. 33, No. 5, first movement (conclusion, mm. 301–5)

e. Beethoven: Symphony No. 8 in F Major, Op. 93, first movement (beginning, mm. 1–2)

f. Beethoven: Symphony No. 8 in F Major, Op. 93, first movement (conclusion, mm. 372–73)

to work with, but he made the most of it. Adding to what Alec Wilder called Rodgers's "perfect" melody, Hart brilliantly realized that his collaborator's imaginative use of the note D-flat deserved to be heard on such "magic" words like "word" (m. 8), "love" (m. 16), and finally sealed with a "kiss" (m. 24).

The song just detailed is the song that has captivated listeners, singers, film directors, and advertisers for more than ninety years. But it's not quite the song heard by viewers of *Love Me Tonight*. This is because when the song was published, also in 1932, aside from the retention of the song's title, Hart added completely new words to the first stanza in response to all the melopoetic nuances of Rodgers's melody.[24] No doubt the second published stanza, which was what Maurice sang in the film, was rewritten because in their original state his words would have come across as somewhat less than suitably romantic for a future princess. Maurice's idea of romance is to marry a woman who will scrub the floor and his back, cook onion soup, and help the population of France by producing a troupe of "kiddies," all the while kissing him every hour. Instead of Hart's setting, Rodgers's striking D-flat to magic words like "word," "love," and "kiss" and the culminating high F also on the word "love," the words in the film that correspond to the notes of Maurice's catchy strain are, respectively, "floor," "back," "troupe," and "owe." Thus the sounds Jeanette hears from her balcony are not Maurice's unromantic demands of the girl he hopes to discover and adore. Instead what she hears in the distant music is a dream sung by a prince riding to her rescue in armor to kiss her hand. Fortunately, in the film Jeanette hears Rodgers's music but not Hart's words, which were altered by the soldiers and removed from the wordless Gypsy melody.

"Isn't It Romantic?" returns on a number of occasions throughout the film as instrumental music that serves as the first of two leitmotivs for the young lovers. Its first repetition appears shortly after we meet Jeanette's Aunts (23:27) and few seconds later when we see Jeanette sleeping (23:54). It next appears as underscoring when Maurice asks the Butler who made his suit (42:08) and again less than a minute later shortly after the next appearance of the Aunts (43:00). The strong association between the tune and the two lovers is realized in the underscoring at the moment Jeanette realizes she loves Maurice ("How foolish I was") (67:18), repeated seconds later as a full instrumental interlude (67:48). Minutes later, Maurice hums one full chorus and half of a second while he measures Jeanette's riding habit. In the final twenty minutes of the film, "Isn't It Romantic?" will be replaced as the central leitmotiv for Maurice and Jeanette by the music of their love duet, "Love Me Tonight."[25]

"Lover" (27:40–28:56)

Conductor's Score, April 21, 1932; No extant record of when Hart's lyrics were sent to the Studio Relations Committee.

The lyrics of "Lover," the other major hit song from the film, were changed even more profoundly in order to make the song less specific than a young woman singing what might be construed as a love song to her horse (although she is actually singing to a potential *human* lover).[26] This time the lyrics share only a single word, "lover," sung four times in both the film and published versions. Not only would such published lyrics as "softly, in my ear you breathe a flame" and "Lover, when we're dancing" appear inappropriate for a woman to sing to a horse, they might be destined for removal by the censors at the Studio Relations Committee. On the other hand, the lyrics she sings to an unknown lover in the film conceivably could have passed the censors even if her lover was within earshot. In any event, it would be clear to the censors as it is to us that when Jeanette expresses her desires for her lover to kiss her and sings that she is looking forward to serving as a slave for her lord and master that the surrogate horse serves as an innocent bystander to her unbridled passions.

In the course of one minute and fourteen seconds Rodgers's first of many well-remembered waltzes (roughly thirty seconds shorter than Chopin's famous minute waltz), Jeanette's horse interrupts her song three times: 1) "With your *glow* make me cast behind me all your *WHOA!*"; 2) "like two children playing in the HEY!"; and 3) "He'll make my heartbeat go fast—NOT TOO FAST!" As mentioned earlier, the song is diegetic. This is not because the horse hears Jeanette's song and interjections, although it does, but because her future lover, Maurice, informs her (and us) that *he* heard her song before her horse and carriage collapsed into a ditch.

The song is in A-A-B-A form but with each letter allotted sixteen bars instead of the customary eight. Within the first ten bars in each of the first two A sections the melody gradually descends a fourth (C down to G) by chromatic half steps, starting with C in the first measure of the published vocal score, B-natural in the second measure, B-flat in the fourth, A in the sixth, A-flat in the ninth, and G in the tenth. The first two A sections are identical, even ending on the same note, a G in the key of C, unusual in a Rodgers song but repeated in "Mimi" which closely follows. The B section (or release) surprises by moving suddenly to an E major chord without the preparation of formal modulation. In this section each phrase begins with a rising rather than a falling half step (G-sharp to A in the first 8 bars and B to C in the second) before culminating with the highest note of the song, the half-step D-sharp to E on the words "to be" followed by a downward leap to G on "mine." In the final A on the words "to my heart," the last three notes of the song, Rodgers returns to the highest note "E" before resolving down a third to a C in the melody as well as a C major harmony. The song will return only once more in the film as instrumental dance music played at the Ball, not unlike its use in the movie *Sabrina.*

"Mimi" (30:34–31:46) and "Mimi" reprise (46:00–48:13)

Conductor's Score, March 11, 1932, and July 27, 1932. Hart's lyrics sent to the Studio Relations Committee on March 19.

When the seamstress Mimi meets the poet Rodolfo in act I of Giacomo Puccini's *La Bohème* (1896), she sings the famous aria "Mi chiamano Mimi" ("They call me Mimi"). Perhaps after Maurice carries a resisting Jeanette out of the ditch and asks whether he can sing for her, the creators of "Mimi," may have been thinking of Puccini's heroine. In any event, the name Mimi is a lot easier to sing than Jeanette.

"Mimi," at one minute and twelve seconds (two seconds shorter than "Lover") is not only a non sequitur, it's insulting ("you funny little good-for-nothing Mimi"), presumptuous ("you know I'd like to have a little son of a Mimi, by and by"), and even lecherous (Chevalier's facial expression when he sings this last lyric). Curiously, the line about Jeanette's impregnation (perhaps out of wedlock) was eliminated when the film was shown in Ontario, Canada, but otherwise didn't seem to perturb the censors at the Studio Relations Committee during the Pre-Production Code era.

When a character announces he or she is going to sing a song, viewers clearly grasp that the principle of diegeticism is at work. In their conversation moments before he starts to sing, Jeanette accuses Maurice of being mad (in addition to pointing out the fact that her name isn't Mimi). Maurice's lyrics in the song's verse confirm his awareness of this madness ("my left shoe's on my right foot" and "of reason I'm bereft"). Given the ubiquity of the form in 1932, it might be surprising to learn that "Mimi"'s chorus exhibits the *first* example in the film so far of a conventional 32-bar A-A-B-A form. The first two A sections are almost identical, including the closing pitches of each (as with "Lover"). A distinctive rhythmic characteristic of the song is that with the exception of the final held note that extends over the final two measures of each A, all the other notes are quarter notes.

It is also striking that of the seventeen notes in each A section, eight of the pitches are D. These include the two statements of Mimi's name that introduce each of the four phrases in these two sections and the long-held D at the end of each A section. The repetition of her name at the beginning of each phrase gives the impression that the name Mimi is not only the beginning of the second phrase but the end of the first phrase. Maurice is mad about Mimi and her name and will sing it as much as possible, not only in each of the four phrases of the first two A sections and the opening of the final A but also to introduce the B section. The harmony supporting the first statements of her name (two quarter note Ds) are G major triads, but Rodgers varies the harmonic support of the other Ds. An interesting harmonic twist of this simple song is that, despite Rodgers's insistence on D (a fifth above the tonic G, i.e., the dominant), which normally would pull to the root of G major (the tonic), the song delays a firm resolution on the home key until the word "son" in the final phrase of the song and again on the concluding held note on "by."

Soon Maurice will arrive at Jeanette's chateau and captivate the Duke, his family, and even the servants. His intelligence, charm, and vitality offer a welcome contrast to the doldrums of the chateau residents, men and women, high and low. The only ones who resist his charms are the Count de Savignac and most importantly Jeanette. There is no evidence that Maurice has sung "Mimi" to anyone else, and it's extremely doubtful that anyone could hear the orchestra play the tune after Gilbert has introduced Maurice as his friend the Baron (45:30). And yet, the first thing the next morning (thirty seconds later in the film), the Duke, Gilbert, the Aunts, and the Count wake up singing "Mimi" with great exuberance, a testament to the charms of Maurice, who has injected new life into the sleepy chateau. Sadly, when the film was rereleased, Myrna Loy's chorus was removed due to a wardrobe malfunction that offended the Production Code Administration's prudish sensibilities (see chapter 5).

In the Buff Script (see Table 1.1), Maurice sings "Mimi" to Jeanette as part of an after-dinner exchange, but by the White Script, the song had attained its rightful place at their initial meeting in the countryside. In the earlier context Maurice sings "Mimi" to all the chateau residents and asks them to join in while the scene directions explain that "Jeanette is still rather sulky."[27]

The Buff Script version may not be as imaginative, but having Maurice sing "Mimi" to the group at least would explain how the Duke, Valentine, Ruggles, the Aunts, and the Count came to know the song they reprise when they wake up the next morning. In the absence of a countryside meeting, Jeanette and Maurice first meet in the Buff Script when the tailor finds the princess in her bedroom trying to write a letter to her girlfriend, and they sing a charming song about it (see the discussion of the discarded "The Man for Me").

"A Woman Needs Something Like That" (34:58–37:57)

Conductor's Score, March 2, 1932; Hart's lyrics sent to the Studio Relations Committee on March 7.

When Jeanette returns to the chateau after meeting Maurice, she falls into a faint and takes to her bed. When Doctor Armond de Pontignac arrives at her bedside to examine her, their rhythmic and rhymed dialogue becomes the starting point for "A Woman Needs Something Like That." It is a song thoroughly integrated into the story, a musical setting of a conversation that occurs in real time. Since the film deleted the preliminary conversation in which Jeanette demands that her Doctor be of noble birth, the first words of the scene viewers hear is the Doctor's startling request for Jeanette to remove her dress. For viewers who had seen MacDonald in previous films, the Doctor's request should probably not have come as too much of a surprise. In fact, MacDonald's biographer Edward Baron Turk informs his readers that "during these Paramount years [1929–1932] MacDonald would sing so many songs in underwear and dressing gowns that music industry insiders soon called her 'the boudoir warbler.'"[28]

The song also reveals considerable information about Jeanette's backstory. In response to the Doctor's questions we learn that she has been experiencing numerous fainting spells (already noted by the three Aunts) and that she feels depressed when she's alone in bed at night. She informs the Doctor she is twenty-two, that she was married at sixteen to a man of seventy-two, and a widow for three years. When she describes her marriage as "happiness of great peace," the orchestra plays the opening of Felix Mendelssohn's "Spring Song," but when she shows the Doctor a photograph of her noble husband and viewers can observe the man she married, Mendelssohn's playful melody metamorphoses into a comical off-key version played by a bass clarinet. The implication is that Princess's marriage was unconsummated and that her nighttime depression is due to sexual deprivation.

In the film version that we have today, after Jeanette sings about wasting away the Doctor concludes that with her figure and beauty she is not wasting away—she's "just wasted." As originally filmed, the Doctor is asked to sing as he explains that just as "a flower needs sprinkling" and "a car needs ignition to keep in condition," "a woman needs something like that," the "something" clearly being sexual satisfaction. Although it's doubtful the Doctor would be singing these lines, even if he were permitted, his final words along with his other sung contribution to the scene were removed by the Studio Relations Committee in 1932.

"A Woman Needs Something Like That" is both more and less than a song. It is a dramatic scene, much of it spoken. The transcription of Rodgers's manuscript in the Conductor's Score indicates that the Doctor did have something to sing ("How old are you," "at twenty-two," "well, it's a very pretty mouth," and "with eyes and red lips and figure like that"), but Joseph Cawthorn, who played the Doctor, doesn't actually sing any of these pitches in the film. Instead, he speaks in the rhythmic dialogue that viewers first heard in the chorus of "The Song of Paree." In contrast, Jeanette sings in three places within the scene. Her first sung words begin with "I feel depressed when I'm alone in bed at night" (eleven seconds beginning at 36:11), and a minute later she sings about how "Sweet music makes me cry and pout" (for another eleven seconds beginning at 37:16). This is the passage Rodgers asks the Doctor to conclude with a clear melodic resolution. Since he doesn't sing it, Rodgers's melody can be heard only in the orchestra. At the end of the song Jeanette also sings her lament that she is wasting away (eight seconds beginning at 37:32).

In a scene lasting three minutes, only thirty seconds are sung. Any of Jeanette's brief but rich musical passages could have been developed into a full-fledged song had Rodgers wanted to (or had been asked to do so by Mamoulian). But even as it stands, the scene is well developed, informative, and carries the drama along in a way that is fulfilling, although it might prove a little unsettling to modern as well as ancient sensibilities. More than any song in Love Me Tonight, "A Woman Needs Something Like That" demonstrates that while the film may be about love and romance, it's also about sex. Even with the removal of the Doctor's original summation, "A Woman Needs Something Like That" makes this point abundantly clear.

"The Poor Apache" (62:00–65:12)

Conductor's Score, April 17, 1932; Hart's lyrics sent to the Studio Relations Committee on April 5.

The January 1932 Treatment (see Table 1.1) suggested that Maurice might entertain the chateau guests after dinner: "This is a good spot to give Chevalier one or two songs or specialties."[29] No song title is provided. In the March Buff Script, the screenwriters identify a song called "The Apache Song" and include a "Note for Mr. Mamoulian" that conveys the problems placing this song in the dramatic flow of the film: "It is difficult, as the play stands at present, to introduce the Apache song. This method is suggested: We see Maurice amid a group of pretty women, guests from outside the chateau."[30]

With his proletarian turtleneck sweater and jacket where others wear a collar and a tie (as he explains in the verse to his song), topped off with a beret, Maurice's attire is deliberately and provocatively out of place among the evening gowns and fancy costumes. Jeanette in particular finds his "common" costume "decidedly" out of place, but Valentine and the Aunts ask Maurice to clarify the misunderstandings people hold about the Apaches and how they relate to women.[31] Maurice obliges them with a song, "The Poor Apache," which gives the chateau residents the opportunity to learn about the Apaches and what they stand for. The lyrics do not, however, address the Apache's origins as members of a "violent criminal underworld subculture of early 20th-century hooligans, night muggers, street gangs and other criminals," who owe their name to "their savagery," which is "attributed by Europeans to the Native American tribes of Apaches."[32]

The lyrics to "The Poor Apache" describe what would today constitute an unacceptable level of violence toward women, going far beyond Maurice's expectations in "Isn't It Romantic?" that his future mate should scratch his back and make onion soup. For example, in the verse Maurice sings, "When I grab her *wrist* and *twist* it no woman can *resist it*" (in case you *missed it* note Hart's internal rhyming in italics). In the chorus he explains that "With one deep *sigh* I must black her *eye!*" The Trio of the song, not included in the published sheet music, goes on to describe the illegitimacy of his birth ("my parents were not well acquainted") and such crimes as "how to pick *pockets* and rob girls of *lockets.*" As with censors and rating systems today, violence, even sexual violence, could be more acceptable in a mainstream motion picture than overt sexuality.

Contributing to the sinister subtext is Mamoulian's decision to insert large and dramatic shadows prominently as backdrops to Maurice's song (see Figure 2.1 and Figure 2.2).

By 1932, the use of shadow-play was a firmly established component of Mamoulian's stage and film work and would remain a familiar stylistic marker in the future. It appears as early as his second production for the American Opera Company in Rochester in December 1923, the prison scene from Gounod's *Faust*, after which Mamoulian used the technique memorably in the saucer burial and hurricane scenes of his first Broadway stage play *Porgy* (1927) and for dramatic effect in his first film, *Applause* (1929).[33] A few years after *Love Me Tonight* Mamoulian used shadow-play to accompany the burial and hurricane scenes in the opera *Porgy and Bess* (1935). In *Love Me Tonight*, shadow-play figures prominently in three places: the Gypsy encampment portion of the "Isn't It Romantic?" montage where shadows visually accompany the violinist who has picked up Maurice's traveling melody from the marching soldiers; on the wall behind the three Aunts as they stir their brew to help cure Jeanette's fainting spells; the large dramatic shadows that loom threateningly behind Maurice as he sings "The Poor Apache."[34]

After disregarding all of the notes Rodgers asks him to sing in the verse (but clearly underscored by the orchestra), Chevalier will sing most of the chorus and trio. Exceptions include the spoken words, "The spot that no one dare touch" [i.e., the derrière] in the B section and the words "I learned how to slouch in doorways and crouch to master a *wench* with a" [spoken] "hammer and *wrench*" [sung], and the second (and final) exclamation of "Oh—nuts to you!" [spoken]. Interestingly, Chevalier makes a melodic alteration (but only one), when he changes the two Gs that ascend to C on "I'm Apache" in the trio to a D that descends to two Cs. Although "The Poor Apache" is mostly in the major mode, it responds to the darkness of the lyrics by exhibiting more than a touch of the minor, most audibly in the second and third measures of the A sections of its standard 32-bar A-A-B-A form (mm. 2–3, 10–11, and 26–27). After an extended Trio (44 bars), the song concludes with one more statement of an A section followed by a four-bar coda.

"The Poor Apache" is thematically related to the Apache *dance* which, like the Apache subculture, can be traced to the earliest years of the twentieth century. Unlike the relationship described in Maurice's song, women in the Apache dance talk and fight back with words, slaps, and punches. This male-female combat is depicted in one of Ernst Lubitsch's three segments in the film revue *Paramount on Parade* (1930), introduced by and starring

Figure 2.1 Filming and recording "The Poor Apache."

Figure 2.2 Maurice Chevalier singing "The Poor Apache."

Chevalier, called "The Real Origin of the Apache." This five-minute classical Pre-Code sequence set to Jacques Offenbach's "Valse des Rayons" from
his ballet *Le Papillon* from 1860 (by 1930 already long associated with the
Apache dance), depicts an argument between a wife (Evelyn Brent) and her
husband (Chevalier) whom she accuses of flirting with another woman.
The accusation becomes a quarrel that leads to mutual slapping, but soon
the slaps are replaced by mutual stripping. The camera shows the discarded

items tossed into the frame one by one, including the wife's underwear, after which we see the now-happy couple leaving their bedroom in evening attire. Rick Altman observes that the Apache dance is a "conflictual, violent affair reputed to be representative of the twin French traits of overt interest in sexuality and a tendency toward violent male domination" and that in this context "fighting is not opposed to sexual activity, according to this myth, it *is* sexual activity."[35] Although the violence as sex trope is one-sided when Maurice sings "The Poor Apache," it's possible to see how Chevalier's Apache dance in *Paramount on Parade* anticipates the later song.

In the early years of sound film, most songs were recorded directly on the set as we can see from Figure 2.1. In the first Chevalier–MacDonald film musical *The Love Parade* (1929), directed by Lubitsch, only the "March of the Grenadiers" was not recorded directly.[36] On set recording would remain the method practiced at Paramount prior to *Love Me Tonight*, although an exception occurs in the second Lubitsch musical, *Monte Carlo* (1930), starring MacDonald without Chevalier, which featured an elaborate and highly regarded film sequence, "Beyond the Blue Horizon" that was not recorded directly on the set.[37] RKO only began using prerecording routinely in *The Gay Divorcee* (1934).[38] After *Love Me Tonight*, prerecorded, dubbed sound became the typical production practice, as it remains to the present day.

Miles Kreuger apparently discussed the recording methods used in *Love Me Tonight* with both Mamoulian and Rodgers. In the Audio Commentary that came with the 2003 DVD, Kreuger recalled Rodgers telling him that most of the songs were not dubbed:

> Dick Rodgers told me that this tradition [i.e., recording on the set] was retained for most of the songs in *Love Me Tonight*. Although it took several days to shoot "Isn't It Romantic?" for example, the vocals were recorded and shot simultaneously with a metronome to keep the timing consistent from one day to the next.[39] He said that it was the complexity of the numbers in this film that convinced the industry that to continue the trend of visual flexibility during production numbers it would be necessary to prerecord and shoot to playback.[40] *42nd Street* was the first major film to do so for its big Busby Berkeley routines a few months later.[41]

Aside from "Love Me Tonight," which was sung by Chevalier and MacDonald in voice-over as we see them sharing a bed in a split-screen, the extent to which the other songs are sung while shooting or prerecording has not been clarified. Kreuger's assertion that most of the songs were sung directly on the set does not negate the need for post-synchronization between the prerecorded sounds of the orchestra with the singers.[42] In the future, the standard practice would have the singers lip-synching to their own prerecordings, but *Love Me Tonight* may indeed offer one of the last vestiges of on-the-set recording. Based on physical evidence, with the exception of "The Poor Apache," the orchestra was probably not in this room at the time.

Mamoulian's description of how "The Song of Paree" was recorded might shed some light on how it is possible, both that the singers are singing directly on the set and that a prerecorded orchestra is dubbing the singer rather than vice versa:

> A young French girl at her window on the top floor puts on a gramophone record—this brings the first music into the scene. Then the orchestra starts coming in softly and keeps building up gradually. Now we cut back to Chevalier in his room. He starts singing. From here on the whole singing sequence was shot to the soft accompaniment of a piano on a set.[43]

But just as it is unequivocally clear that "Love Me Tonight" was prerecorded, Figure 2.1 clearly displays the fact that Chevalier not only recorded "The Poor Apache" directly on the set but that he did it in the presence of a live orchestra.

"Love Me Tonight" (71:15–72:17)

Conductor's Score, March 7, 1932; Hart's lyrics sent to the Studio Relations Committee on March 9.

By the time Maurice and Jeanette are ready to sing their big love song in duple meter, "Love Me Tonight," both film viewers and the lovers on the screen have heard their melody about a minute earlier as a waltz (the music of love and romance in triple meter) that underscores their pledge. Rodgers's score, the Conductor's Score, and the published vocal score all include a verse omitted in the White and Release Scripts and the film itself. When Colonel Jason S. Joy at the Studio Relations Committee responded to B. P. ("Budd") Schulberg at Paramount on March 12 a few days after receiving Hart's lyrics, he found the line "Must we sleep tonight all alone?" questionable but permissible. In response, on March 16 Paramount's Jesse L Lasky offered "Let's drink deep tonight all alone" as a possible substitution, perhaps without consulting Hart. When the entire verse was discarded, the point became moot.

As filmed and published, the song consists of a single stanza that takes just over a minute to sing. Such succinctness makes the title song one of three songs (out of the eight total) that quickly come and go. As with "The Poor Apache," but without a verse or a trio, "Love Me Tonight" is a 32-bar song form (A-A-B-A). Jeanette sings the first two A sections, Maurice the release and the final A, the latter harmonized by his Princess.

Although the melody is simple, it satisfies everything one might ask of a central love song. Of special interest is the way words and music capture the title at the end of each A section, a total of three times occupying eleven of the 32 total measures. As if in response to Jeanette's plea that her heart and Maurice's heart shouldn't be made to wait, the words and music arrive without waiting for the first statement of the title set to a swift "love me to-" and a long "night." By the time Jeanette sings the word "love" the second time, the music has already arrived on the highest note of the song, an E followed by another E on the "to-" of "tonight."

The final statement of "love me tonight" preserves the melodic (one octave) and rhythmic spaciousness of the second "love me tonight" (long held notes) albeit one note lower. The dramatic high E returns, but this time it is heard for five beats on the word "sings." This climax on "sings" suggests to listeners that they hear the final words "love me tonight" as a peaceful denouement. By this time viewers have had ample opportunity to see the two lovers in bed thanks to the use of a split screen. It was unusual for a love song at the time on stage or screen to be sung in voice-over and would remain so. A famous later example is "Twin Soliloquies" from Rodgers and Hammerstein's *South Pacific* (stage 1949; film 1958). The combination of film and sound in "Love Me Tonight" is not only effective artistically, it also serves as a clever way to circumvent the censors at the Studio Relations Committee in 1932 and later the Production Code Administration.

Rodgers captures the rising trajectory of love by moving expansively and ever upward in the first A rising by thirds from D to F (m. 1), F to A (m. 2), up to C in bars 3–5. The second A rises still higher from D to F to A to C (mm. 9–12) before reaching the high note E on "love" (bars 13–14). In the B section Rodgers employs one of his musical trademarks: the simple but versatile scale.[44] As if in answer to the rising four-note scale on the first statement of "love me tonight" at the end of the first A section (mm. 6-8), the release consists of two four-note sequentially descending scales (D-C-B-A and

C-B-A-G) as if to mark the uncertainty of the question, "Who knows what tomorrow brings with the morning light?" With the word "light" following a leap after "morning," Rodgers firmly resolves to the tonic, the first phrase to do so at the end of a section.

The importance of "Love Me Tonight" to the romantic trajectory of the Princess and the tailor inspires wonder that the Treatment of January 18 seriously considered giving this song to Valentine. During the film's remaining minutes viewers will have ample opportunity to hear the title song again. Not only will Jeanette hear Maurice sing the first two A sections of the chorus in her mind as a voice-over, she will finish the song, just as viewers witness Maurice leave the chateau to catch the train to Paris. Directly following the song is an instrumental reprise consisting of one chorus plus an additional A section. This is followed by no fewer than five additional A-A-B-A choruses heard as underscoring as Jeanette races on her horse to stop Maurice's train.

"The Son-of-a-Gun Is Nothing but a Tailor" (80:58–83:13)

Conductor's Score, February 16, 1932; Hart's lyrics sent to the Studio Relations Committee on February 19.

"The Son-of-a-Gun Is Nothing but a Tailor" is a nondiegetic but thoroughly integrated dramatic scene framed by a song. For *New York Times* reviewer Mordaunt Hall, the filming of this song revealed Mamoulian "at the height of his form," and the more the upstairs and downstairs chateau residents sing (or speak) the song's title "the more one wants to hear it."[45] And like the reprise of "Mimi" and the spectacular montage that accompanied "Isn't It Romantic?" "Son-of-a-Gun" might also be thought of as a passed-along or traveling song as the shocking revelation spreads through the chateau. It begins with the Duke, who is so shocked at the news that he'd "rather throw a bomb in her [i.e., his niece Jeanette], than have her wed a commoner."[46] Although Rodgers provides specific pitches, the opening section of the scene is mostly declaimed in rhythmic and rhymed speech in the manner of "A Woman Needs Something Like That." After the Duke's extended outburst we hear snippets as brief as "a tailor!" from Valentine and the Second Aunt, followed by a few words more from the Third Aunt and the Count before the Duke reenters to remark that if the picture of his ancestor could hear this damning news "his frame would crash off the wall."[47] Right on cue, the picture fulfills the Duke's prediction and crashes to the floor, after which it (yes, the picture in the frame) sings the song title in a *basso profundo* timbre and pitchless monotone to comic effect. When the picture is finished, the three Aunts successively bark a high-pitched exclamation "Oh!" that sounds like a small dog, each bark squarely on the downbeat followed by a Pomeranian pup, whose bark is virtually indistinguishable from that of the Aunts. After one more monotonal (but on pitch) statement of the song's title, the Butler rushes to the kitchen to break the news to the supercilious downstairs staff.

The sung portion of the scene begins. Its melody is set in a simple 32-bar A-A-B-A form in which the first A ends on an open-ended pitch and the second and fourth A sections firmly close with the root D of the tonic D major in both the Conductor's Score and the film. Each chorus takes exactly thirty seconds. The simple outline below shows how the song is doled out to the various shocked and angry servants. With the exception of the Valet, who adopts rhythmic speech, all the other servants sing Rodgers's notes:

> First Chorus (81:51)
> A A Butler
> B A Valet
> Second Chorus (82:21)
> A A Chambermaid
> B A Chef[48]
> Third Chorus (82:51)
> A A B A Laundress

The anger and class-conscious snobbery of the servants is cleverly conveyed in Hart's lyrics. The Valet complains that he should have blacked Maurice's eye instead of his boots and is struck by the fact that he *pressed* Maurice's coat and *vest* when "he's the one who can press the *best.*" The Chambermaid regrets that she "used to *flirt* until it *hurt* while he stood there in his *undershirt.*" The Chef finds it hard to imagine "cooking *pheasant* for a guy who's just a *peasant.*" The Laundress complains about the fact that she had to work on her "hands and *kneeses* washing out his B-V-*D'ses*," "a job that hardly *pleases.*"

The song emphasizes the magnitude of the outrage of Maurice's newly discovered professional identity by repeating, as if in disbelief, the song's title at the end of each A section for a total of nine times in the course of three choruses, still not enough for Mordaunt Hall. At the end of the song, Jeanette speaks the last four words of the song title "nothing but a tailor" twice, and a chorus of chateau residents and even the wall whisper the travesty of the song's full title another eight times.

Songs that Didn't Make the Cut

Prior to the Buff Script some songs given titles and dramatic situations were abandoned before reaching completion: "It's Only Eighty Rooms but It's a Home" and "Sailor Song" in the Skeleton (January 8) (3); "What Could I Do?" and "I Find This Much Simpler and Nicer" in the Treatment (January 18) (Sequence C, 13 and Sequence D, 14).

- "Give Me Just a Moment" [lyrics only extant]

Since scholars have yet to discover a Hart lyric without a corresponding Rodgers melody, it is reasonable to surmise that Rodgers composed the music for Hart's lyric "Give Me Just a Moment" and that the music was lost.[49] In the Rouben Mamoulian Collection, Library of Congress, the lyrics to this song also include sufficiently detailed scene descriptions to conclude that this was the "Untitled" song described in the Treatment (Sequence F, 21–22).[50] It is also likely that this song was a discarded version of what would become "Love Me Tonight," which appears in the film narrative about the same place in the March Buff Script.

Both Jeanette and Maurice are experiencing a sleepless night. When Jeanette finally succumbs to the arms of Morpheus, she dreams of Maurice who appears as an armored knight singing a love song. Meanwhile, when Maurice finally manages to sleep, he dreams of returning to Jeanette from a day's work, and they make love instead of eating the dinner she has prepared. In his dream he knocks a coffee pot off the table. At that precise moment in real life, the sleeping Maurice knocks a candle off his bed table. By now fully awake, Jeanette and Maurice go to their respective bedroom windows and alternate phrases of a love song accompanied by external sounds of nature and indoor synchronized sounds, including the snoring Duke and Aunts and various clocks throughout the chateau. In the film, Jeanette and Maurice, who express their love in person while awake earlier that night, are seen peacefully sleeping side by side (but modestly in the privacy of their respective bedrooms) while their respective voice-overs of "Love Me Tonight" alternate as they did in the abandoned and forgotten "Give Me Just a Moment."

- "The Man for Me" [music and lyrics completed but deleted after filming]

The song matching the description of "The Man for Me," labeled "Letter Song" in the various script drafts, made its first appearance in the March Buff Script (Sequence C, 112). By then, it had been copied as a piano-vocal score by Paramount on February 17 (although unlike the copies used in the film it is not labeled Conductor's Score on its first page). Its lyrics had been sent for review to the Studio Relations Committee on February 19 and "registered for copyright as an unpublished song by Famous Music" on February 29.[51] The song was not only completed but also shot before it was removed from the film.[52] Since Colonel Joy of the SRC wrote to Budd Schulberg at Paramount on February 22 that the lyrics "are satisfactory under the Code and that they contain nothing reasonably censorable," the song's removal was probably due either to the need to curtail the running time or to dissatisfaction with the song itself.[53]

While not a catastrophe, the removal of "The Man for Me" might be considered a loss, since it is the only time Jeanette and Maurice get to know each other in song. In some ways it presages the conditional love duets Rodgers would later compose to Hammerstein's lyrics such as "People Will Say We're in Love" from *Oklahoma!* (1943) and "If I Loved You" from *Carousel* (1945). But although it has something in common with these future songs, it probably is more similar to the earlier "Make Believe" from *Show Boat* (1927)—lyrics by Hammerstein and music by Kern—in which Magnolia and Ravenal meet for the first time and pretend they are actors playing a part of a couple in love. In the absence of "Lover" and "Mimi," which occupy a later position in the Buff Script, "The Man for Me" also serves as the *first* planned meeting of the future lovers. In the White and Release scripts "The Man for Me" took place at their second meeting. In both scripts, while roaming the chateau looking for Gilbert, Maurice discovers Jeanette in her room writing a letter to a girlfriend to whom she has nothing to say. "The Man for Me" is also a net loss because unlike anything else in the film, it presents a true *musical* conversation (albeit intermixed with some underscored conversation mainly in the beginning). "A Woman Needs Something Like That" offers a conversation, just not a musical one, and besides, it does not involve both future lovers.

In this little discarded musical scene, Maurice offers to help Jeanette compose her letter and Jeanette agrees.[54] He then takes advantage of this opportunity by dictating a letter in which she tells her friend she has "met the one man" for her and extolling his virtues. The song becomes more humorous when Maurice asks Jeanette to read what he has dictated. Instead of expressing her delight and passion in meeting the new visitor, she instead pretends to read a letter in which she describes Maurice as "a foolish young man," "undistinguished and *plain*," "unattractive yet *vain*," and concluding with a final verdict that "he is not the man for her." Although Jeanette and Maurice will meet and find their way to love by the end of the film, the removal of "The Man for Me" meant that Maurice cannot credibly discover Jeanette as he roams the chateau to the music of "How Are You?" In the balance more seems lost than gained by the removal of this musically and dramatically rich three-minute scene between the tailor and the Princess, and it's a shame the footage seems to be permanently lost.

Closing Thoughts

"Lover" may have been "one of six best sellers in the country" as Rodgers wrote to Dorothy in June 1933, and "Isn't It Romantic?" may be distinguished as the earliest song to make the list of 100 songs in AFI's *100 Years . . . 100 Songs*.[55] But in their own time Rodgers and Hart fell short in the contest that determined the dozen most popular songs to debut in Paramount musicals from 1929 to 1933. The music to three of the twelve was composed by Richard A. Whiting alone and another two by Whiting in collaboration with another composer. Five songs had lyrics by Leo Robin and three had lyrics by Sam Coslow. Only one Rodgers and Hart song made the list, "Isn't It Romantic?"

In addition to "Isn't It Romantic?" probably no more than three others from this list of a dozen are remembered today. One of these is "Louise," a Whiting–Robin collaboration that appeared in *Innocents of Paris* (1929), a sensationally popular film in its day but now forgotten.[56] This was the song (as well as the film) that put Chevalier on the map and led to a lucrative five-year Paramount contract and perhaps the chief reason everyone in 1932 described *Love Me Tonight* as a "Chevalier picture." "Louise" was the

most popular song of Paramount's early years producing sound films, sel-
ling 100,000 copies more than the next nearest hit. Sales of the other two
not-yet-forgotten songs from these dozen hits, "Dream Lover" (music by
Victor Schertzinger and lyrics by Clifford Grey) from *The Love Parade* and
"Beyond the Blue Horizon" (music by W. Franke Harling and Whiting) from
Monte Carlo, fell far below "Louise"'s 385,000 copies. In fact, neither "Dream
Lover" nor "Beyond the Blue Horizon" sold many more copies of sheet music
than the eleventh greatest hit on this short list at 37,266 copies.[57]

The No. 11 hit between 1929 and 1933, which nosed out No. 12 by barely
a thousand copies, was "Isn't It Romantic?" As Allison Robbins concludes,
"*Love Me Tonight* may have been a critical darling, but the bottom line was
that Rodgers and Hart did not produce a mega-hit for the studio."[58] But
while the score to *Love Me Tonight* may have lacked the contemporary appeal of "Louise," it is to be hoped that this chapter has revealed its much-
deserved popularity and critical acclaim, especially of "Lover" and "Isn't It
Romantic?" In addition, "Mimi" and "Love Me Tonight," also-rans in their
day, have long since taken an honored place among the pillars of the Great
American Songbook, and Rodgers and Hart's score for *Love Me Tonight* as a
whole continues to be regarded as one of most melodic, cleverest, and memorable of all film musical scores.

3

Rodgers the Musical "Auteur"

Instrumental Numbers, Leitmotivs, Borrowings, Allusions, and Underscoring

"One sequence I was particularly proud of was the scoring for the deer hunt. In it I had to create two contrasting and intercutting themes, one—on the brass—for the pursuing dogs and horses, the other—on the strings—for the frightened deer. Mamoulian staged the entire sequence as if it were a zoological ballet."

Richard Rodgers, *Musical Stages*, 149.

Rodgers's Demanding Musical Assignment

The first chapter of this Guide noted the passage in Rodgers's autobiography, *Musical Stages*, where the composer expressed his gratitude to director Rouben Mamoulian for sharing his (and Hart's) cinematic vision. At the heart of this vision was the belief "that a musical film should be created in musical terms—that dialogue, song and scoring should all be integrated as closely as possible so that the final product would have a unity of style and design."[1] Fortunately, since Mamoulian was also the film's producer, he not only enjoyed "complete autonomy," he was in a position to develop the mutual goals he shared with Rodgers and Hart into an imaginatively stylized reality.

Mamoulian's demanding instrumental musical assignments for Rodgers, which went far beyond the usual job description for a songwriter in a film musical, and Rodgers's creative response to these demands, provides the subjects of this chapter. To refresh memories, here again is Rodgers explaining Mamoulian's demands and the composer's response:

Love Me Tonight. Geoffrey Block, Oxford University Press. © Oxford University Press 2024.
DOI: 10.1093/9780197566220.003.0003

> One of the first things he [Mamoulian] insisted on was that I compose all
> the background music, not simply the music for the songs. This was—and
> is—highly unusual, since film scoring has generally been left to composers
> specializing in the field. It is more or less stopwatch composing, with the
> writer creating musical themes to fit precisely into a prescribed number of
> frames. I had no background in this sort of work but I found it extremely
> challenging and fun to do, and it certainly helped giving the film the desired
> creative unity.[2]

What Mamoulian was asking Rodgers to do was nothing less than to compose the music for an entire film score, including the self-contained instrumental numbers. The assignment included (but was not limited to) what is
frequently the most ubiquitous musical component of a film musical other
than the songs: the underscoring. Underscoring is the term film (and theater) practitioners and scholars use to identify the music that may appear
prominently in the foreground (to accompany a kiss, for example), but more
typically serves as "background music" (Rodgers's term) underneath spoken
dialogue. *Love Me Tonight* reverses these proportions. Although music does
sometimes underscore dialogue, more commonly it accompanies visual
elements that precede or follow dialogue.

Instead of delegating the underscoring and the major self-contained instrumental music to studio staff composers and arrangers, Mamoulian assigned
these tasks to Rodgers. Since the handwritten drafts and Conductor's Score
for this material housed in the Paramount Archives are not in Rodgers's hand,
however, it is difficult to determine the extent of his involvement in serving
Mamoulian's request and thus to determine the extent to which Rodgers was
a musical "auteur" beyond writing the songs.[3] Based on Rodgers's autobiography and our knowledge of his technical skills as a musician, it is not a
stretch to credit Rodgers as the composer of the leitmotivs and central thematic material for the "Hunt."[4] On the other hand, it is less likely that he was
responsible for supplying the details of synchronization between music and
footage in the latter, which in any event was not worked out until several
months after Rodgers completed his work on the songs.[5]

In fulfilling this demanding additional musical component, and presumably in consultation with Mamoulian (certainly with his acquies-
cence), Rodgers conceived a small group of themes to represent human
characters, animals, and activities such as life on the crowded streets of Paris
or sewing a tapestry. Not counting the numerous glimpses of a deer and the

dogs that chase it in "The Hunt," each animal with its own theme, Rodgers came up with seven themes, most of which will appear between two and six times during the course of the film. No fewer than five of these themes are introduced in the Prelude ("Myrna's Theme," "Duke Theme," "Aunts Theme," "Camera Theme," and "Street Scene Tune"), which lasts barely over a minute.[6] The "Ruggles" and "Butler" themes will follow when the narrative begins. Rodgers himself only specified the "Aunts Theme" in his manuscript, but with the exception of the "Street Scene Tune," the Conductor's Score offers titles for the other themes ("Myrna's Theme," "Duke Theme," and "Camera Theme"), all of which were added in cursive writing.

In contrast to the rich thematic family network found in Richard Wagner's *Ring* cycle, Rodgers's themes are not organized into musical families, nor do they undergo the kind of complex musical transformations that populate the operas of Wagner or the operas and tone poems of Richard Strauss. Instead, in quantity and treatment they more closely resemble the "reminiscence" themes found in the operas of Giuseppe Verdi and many other composers, for example the "kiss" and "jealousy" themes in *Otello* (1887).[7]

The term widely used for these recurring themes is leitmotiv. Many films and musicals as well as operas have them. A highpoint of this practice perhaps occurred two decades after *Love Me Tonight* when composer Leonard Bernstein in *West Side Story* (1957) used leitmotivs (and their transformations) for dramatic as well as musical advantage.[8] In *Love Me Tonight* the four themes based on characters ("Aunts Theme," "Duke Theme," "Ruggles Theme," and "Butler Theme") invariably appear in the orchestra, virtually unchanged, to accompany the appearance of the character in the film. Three additional leitmotivs either appear one time only ("Myrna's Theme") or do not directly coincide with specific characters ("Street Scene Tune" and "Camera Theme").[9]

Another musical category is musical borrowing and allusion. There are ten borrowings and allusions in all.[10] Most of these would likely be familiar to film audiences in 1932, and some might be familiar to modern viewers as well. The borrowings and allusions, all heard in the first two-thirds of the film (from 3:48 to 59:00), each serve a particular dramatic purpose. The earliest composed are Wolfgang Amadeus Mozart's popular Minuet from the act 1 Finale of *Don Giovanni* (1787) and the French Revolutionary song "Ça Ira" from 1790. The remaining borrowings and allusions use nineteenth- century sources with the exception of a nod to a contemporary George Gershwin work from 1931.

In several cases the borrowings and allusions offer a shortcut. For example, instead of trying to create a pseudo-Strauss waltz of his own to serve as atmospheric ballroom music, Rodgers, Broadway's "waltz king," was content to borrow the waltz *Thousand and One Nights* (1871) by operetta's "waltz king" Johann Strauss Jr. to accompany dancing and underscore conversation for the chateau ball following the hunt. Another familiar melody is the rousing "There'll Be a Hot Time in the Old Town Tonight" (1896), now parodied with a lugubriously slow rendition (marked "Hot Time Olla [*sic*] Dirge"). This musical characterization vividly embodies the decrepitude of the endlessly boring bridge games the Duke and his ancient guests play before Maurice the tailor arrives to collect his money from Count Gilbert and in the process livens things up and wins everyone over. See table 3.1 for a complete list of all the borrowings and allusions.

Introducing the Leitmotivs: The Prelude to *Love Me Tonight*

(C to F major) (0:31–1:41)

Like an overture to an opera or musical, albeit far more compressed, the Prelude to *Love Me Tonight* "sets the stage" for the film to come. The Prelude underscores the appearance of the film logo and title, "A Paramount Picture," followed by the Main Title, major cast members, and other credits. After 101 seconds the film action begins.

Rodgers left the orchestration to John Leipold (1888–1970), and it is not known whether he offered specific requests to Leipold concerning instrumentation such as the use of hand cymbals to emphasize the long-held, and then simply long, dissonant chords that fall dramatically on the off-beat after chromatically rising bass notes (C to C-sharp to D) followed by other bass notes.[11] At 0:42 the score introduces the catchy "Street Scene Tune" discussed in connection with "The Song of Paree" in chapter 2 (Musical Example 2.1). This is the tune based on the whole-tone scale, the scale associated with the French composer Claude Debussy several decades earlier. In the Prelude, the "Street Scene Tune" coincides with the Main Title. The remaining fifty seconds of the Prelude introduces the four previously mentioned leitmotivs, all of which are identified in the Conductor's Score dated July 29, 1932.

Table 3.1 Borrowings and Allusions (in order of appearance)

1:25 "Spinning Song," from *Songs without Words (Lieder ohne Worte)* for piano, Book VI, Op. 67, No. 4 (1843–45), music by Felix Mendelssohn (1809–1847)
  After its introduction in the Prelude, this possible allusion will return with each appearance of the "Camera Theme" (18:50, 19:38, and 70:32), the first of these reappearances as the camera enters the Aunts' tower and the last as it enters Maurice's bedroom.

3:48 "Wintergreen for President" from *Of Thee I Sing* (1931), lyrics by Ira Gershwin (1896–1983), music by George Gershwin (1898–1937)
  First heard at the conclusion of "Symphony of Noises" this allusion is followed by several appearances in the Street Scene that follow

11:19 "Wedding March" from *A Midsummer Night's Dream* (1826) (in triple meter), music by Felix Mendelssohn

21:16 "There'll Be a Hot Time in the Old Town Tonight" ("a la dirge") (1896), lyrics by Joe Hayden, music by Theodore August Metz (1848–1936)

26:04 "Ça Ira" ("It'll Be Fine") (1790), lyrics by Ladré, music by Bécourt

34:00 (approximately), "La Marseillaise" (1792), lyrics and music by Claude Joseph Rouget de Lisle (1760–1836) (first eight measures) [deleted from the completed film][a]

36:49 "Spring Song," from *Songs without Words (Lieder ohne Worte)* for piano, Book V, Op. 62, No. 6 (1842), music by Felix Mendelssohn

39:53 "Minuet" from the act I Finale of *Don Giovanni* (1786), music by Wolfgang Amadeus Mozart (1756–1791)

41:28 "Hail, Hail, the Gang's All Here" from *The Pirates of Penzance* by Gilbert and Sullivan (1879), new lyrics by D. A. Esrom (pseudonym for Theodora Morse [1883–1953]) published in 1917, music by Arthur Sullivan (1842–1900); piccolo solo in the second phrase at 41:42.

52:57 "Pizzicato" movement from *Sylvia* (1876), music by Leo Delibes (1836–1891) (52:57–53:32)
  This allusion to Delibes's ballet (not a borrowing) occurs six times in what Rodgers referred to as his "zoological ballet," "The Hunt": the first five statements are derived from the rhythm, pizzicato articulation, and several pitches of the opening of the movement; the sixth statement is derived from the rhythm of the conclusion of the movement). See appendix 2 for more specific timings.

59:00 *Thousand and One Nights,* Op. 346 (1871), music by Johann Strauss Jr. (1825–1899) Underscoring at the "The Ball."

---

[a] The borrowing was heard when the doctor introduces himself at "Doctor Pierre de Pontignac, a noble family, and now I'm at my ease" (right before he asks Jeanette to remove her dress). Since this portion of the scene was deleted from the finished film, 34:00 is an approximate time.

"Myrna's Theme" (0:49)

The orchestral indication for "Myrna's Theme" includes "viols [violins] trem [tremolo], w.w. [woodwinds], and piano, and the tempo indication "Slow but in Easy Swinging Tempo." The eight-measure theme is of course named after Myrna Loy, who played the man-hungry Valentine. It begins with a stepwise melody consisting of descending and ascending half-steps in its first two measures (E–E-flat–D in measure 1 and C-sharp up to D in measure 2, repeated exactly in measures 5–6). Measures 2 and 6–8 also contain syncopated rhythms. As previously mentioned, the designation "Myrna's Theme" is entered in large cursive letters in the Conductor's Score but not in the copyist's draft score. Curiously, although the character Valentine figures prominently in the film, the Prelude marks the *only* occurrence of "Myrna's Theme."

"Duke Theme" (1:05)

The appearance of the "Duke Theme" in the Prelude is accompanied by a fanfare for "Quassi [*sic*] Toy Trumpets (must be precisely together"). The "Duke Theme" will return without the simultaneous trumpet fanfare three more times in the film with wide gaps between each occurrence (19:58, 43:07, 75:14). Its second appearance comes in 19:58, shown in Musical Example 3.1, where it immediately follows statements of the "Camera Theme" (18:50), "Aunts Theme" (19:06) [Ex. 3.2], and a return of the "Camera Theme" (19:38) [Ex. 3.3] before the "Butler Theme" completes this theme parade at 20:28 (Ex. 3.5).

The third statement of the "Duke Theme" at 43:07 follows seven seconds of "Isn't It Romantic?" and its final appearance at 75:14 directly precedes

Musical Example 3.1 "Duke Theme" (19:58)

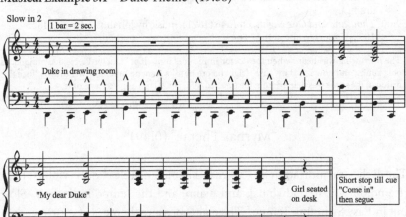

Maurice's humming reprise of "Isn't It Romantic?" as he measures Jeanette for her new riding habit.

During its second and third appearances (19:58 and 43:07), both without the trumpet fanfare heard in the Prelude, the eight measures of the "Duke Theme" demonstrate the character of a march. In the first four bars (two bars repeated) a unison bass line in accented quarter notes gradually ascends from D up to B-flat on the strong beats (D–E–G–B-flat) and keeps returning to C on the off-beats. The chords of the march's second half support the simplest of melodies (four C's, all half notes, and seven F's, all quarter notes). The final appearance at 75:14 concludes abruptly with an unresolved diminished seventh.

"Aunts Theme" (1:14)

Not only is the "Aunts Theme" the only theme that the unknown copyist indicates on the handwritten draft score, it is also the only title that is printed rather than added in cursive writing (usually "Aunts Theme," one time as "Aunt's Theme," and never "Aunts' Theme).

Aside from the seven statements of the deer and the dog themes in "The Hunt," the "Aunts" leitmotiv is the most frequently heard leitmotiv, five times after the Prelude (19:09, 23:27, 42:27, 45:00, and 88:29).

Since it also recurs over the longest time span of any leitmotiv, "Aunts Theme," like the characters it represents, provides a connecting link for the film as a whole. Its first appearance after the Prelude at 19:09 is heard between two statements of the "Camera Theme" (the theme, as we will soon see, associated with the sewing of the Aunts' tapestry). A few minutes later at 23:27 the "Aunts Theme" directly precedes a short instrumental reprise of "Isn't It Romantic?" When the melody appears for the fourth time (42:27), it is sandwiched between two brief instrumental excerpts from "Isn't It Romantic?" again emphasizing the connection between the Aunts and the romance between Maurice and Jeanette. Its fifth appearance at 45:00 directly precedes an instrumental statement of "Mimi," the last music heard before the bird calls that wake up the chateau residents to sing a reprise of this tune the next morning. The Aunts final appearance at 88:29 is heard at the beginning of the End Title. The eccentric Aunts truly serve as a musical as well as dramatic through line from Prelude to coda.

Musical Example 3.2 "Aunts Theme" (19:09)

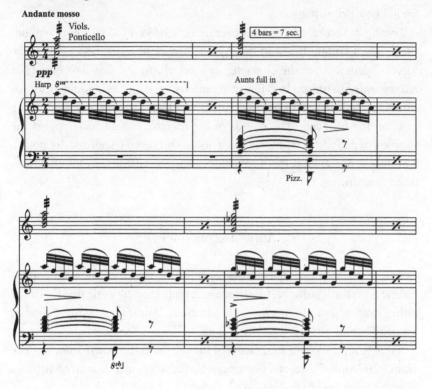

The "Aunts Theme" consists of sustained chords in the upper strings most often with the marking [*sul*] *"ponticello"* (on the bridge). Simultaneously in the upper register Rodgers composes a continuous pattern of sixteenth notes that outline various triads and sevenths throughout. The remaining entrances of the "Aunts Theme" preserve these musical characteristics.

• "Camera Theme" (1:25)

The name "Camera Theme" seems to be derived from the fact that the theme usually accompanies the movement of a camera over the outside of the chateau on its way up either to the tower where the Aunts are sewing their version of a fairy tale ending on a tapestry or in one case into Maurice's bedroom. In Leipold's orchestration of this theme the rapid sixteenth-note figure is played on the strings while the main melody of the theme is given to the harp, piano, and unspecified woodwinds. The sixteenth-note figure suggests the whirring of a motion picture camera. When combined with the eighth-note melody it supports, it also approximates the texture and overall musical character of Felix Mendelssohn's popular "Spinning Song" (1843–45).

The appearance of the "Camera Theme" at 19:38 in the Conductor's Score, six bars after the instruction "dissolve to Castle," contains the direction "camera pans forward." This rubric supports the idea that the theme's labeling was in response to various panning and dissolving camera actions rather than tapestry sewing (or spinning), but the allusion to Mendelssohn's famous piano piece seems likely.

Since the "Camera Theme" on two occasions precedes the appearance of the Aunts as they sew their tapestry, the designation "Sewing Theme" might be more precise than "Camera Theme." If the allusion to the "Spinning Song" is perceived as a credible one, it would join the two unmistakable Mendelssohn quotations, the "Wedding March" and "Spring Song" (see "Borrowings and Allusions," table 3.1). Like the "Duke Theme," the "Camera Theme" will also return three more times (18:50, 19:38, 70:32), twice in virtual succession on either side of the "Aunts Theme" and the one entering Maurice's bedroom directly following the "Love Me Tonight Waltz." The final statement appears immediately prior to Jeanette and Maurice's love duet, "Love Me Tonight."

Musical Example 3.3 "Camera Theme" (19:38)

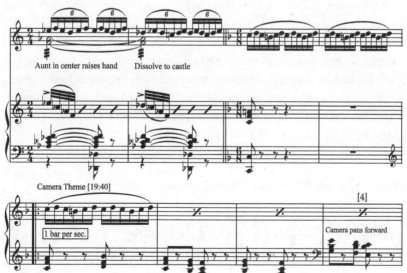

"Street Scene Tune" (1:34)

The Prelude ends almost where it began with a single statement of the "Street Scene Tune" which also supported the first appearance of the Main Title. The "Street Scene Tune" (see Musical Example 2.1) will form the basis of the "Street Scene" that follows and occurs numerous times in "A Song of Paree" (see chapter 2). What happens next to the "Street Scene" music is discussed later in this chapter.

"Ruggles Theme" and "Butler Theme"

"Ruggles Theme"

Leaving aside the many repetitions of the deer and dog leitmotivs that appear exclusively in "The Hunt," the only leitmotivs missing from the Prelude are the "Ruggles Theme" and the "Butler Theme." Appropriately, viewers first hear the "Ruggles Theme" (see Musical Example 3.4), named for Charlie Ruggles who plays Gilbert, Vicomte de Varèze, the first time the actor appears. After running down the street in his t-shirt and boxer trunks, Gilbert (Ruggles) is ducking into Maurice's tailor shop to pick up a suit.

This happens at 8:41 shortly after the "How Are You Interlude," which immediately followed "The Song of Paree." Upon entering Maurice's shop in his underwear, Gilbert explains that the husband of a paramour came home unexpectedly, forcing Gilbert to take flight to escape the husband's wrath. By coincidence, he found himself in an actual foot race. The fast tempo and continuous eighth-note rhythm of his theme captures the act of running, but there are also occasional rests in the principal melody suggesting moments where Gilbert can take a breath. The second appearance of the "Ruggles Theme" (shown in Musical Example 3.4) occurs when Gilbert arrives at the chateau to ask his uncle, the Duke, for a loan (21:48).

Musical Example 3.4 "Ruggles Theme" (21:48)

This second appearance of the "Ruggles Theme" follows directly after the contrasting satiric dirge-like quotation of "There'll Be a Hot Time in the Old Town Tonight," heard as we see the chateau residents enjoying their "hot time" by playing a lugubrious slow game of bridge. "Ruggles" partially returns in two or three further spurts between sections of dialogue, such as when Gilbert joins the conversation about Jeanette's fainting spell upon her return to the chateau after her initial countryside meeting with Maurice. This is the dialogue that leads to Valentine's widely quoted response, "Bring him right in," when Gilbert asks if she can go for a doctor. After this third incomplete appearance, the "Ruggles Theme" will disappear for the remaining hour left in the film. The demise of his theme might be because it is so closely associated with running that it wouldn't make sense to return to it to describe his less frenetic (albeit impoverished) state in the chateau.

"Butler Theme"

The last leitmotiv to consider is "Butler Theme," which appears twice (20:28 and 42:03) (see Musical Example 3.5). The first appearance occurs at the end of a series of leitmotivs in quick succession ("Camera Theme," "Aunts Theme," "Camera Theme," and "Duke Theme"). The "Butler Theme" first appears when the Duke summons Major Domo Flamand to present the new less-than-youthful footmen for the Duke's approval, which prompts Valentine to remark, "Can't we get any footmen under 40" (added in cursive writing at the end of "Butler Theme" in the Conductor's Score). After hearing Valentine's lament the Duke proclaims, "They'll do, Flamand".

The butler identified by the "Butler Theme" is played by Robert Greig, who was frequently typecast in this profession. The typecasting began when he played a butler in the Marx Brothers' *Animal Crackers* on stage in 1928 and again when it was filmed in 1930, marking Greig's film debut.[12] The "Butler Theme," which lasts only a few seconds, is in C major with quarter notes on C and G in the bass and a simple stepwise melody, all triads, beginning and ending on a C-major triad.

Musical Example 3.5 "Butler Theme" (20:28)

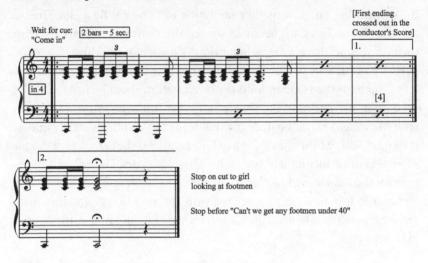

"Symphony of Noises" (street sounds) (1:42–3:57)

Perhaps no portion of *Love Me Tonight* has received more attention than the "Symphony of Noises" that directly follows the Prelude. After acknowledging in *Musical Stages* that "this was entirely Rouben's idea," Rodgers, like many others, compares the opening of *Love Me Tonight* with a scene in the play *Porgy* (1927) by Dorothy and DuBose Heyward, a play not coincidentally directed by Mamoulian. After describing the Parisian adaptation of this scene in Catfish Row, South Carolina, Rodgers asked rhetorically, "Is there any wonder that Larry and I were stimulated by a man as brilliant as Mamoulian?"[13]

The famous opening scene in *Love Me Tonight* begins in the morning as the Parisian streets gradually come to life. In the "symphony of noises" that lasts just over two minutes, viewers see and hear considerable human activity along with some exterior objects such as chimney stacks (using the new device of zoom photography) and storefronts. The post-synchronization of prerecorded sounds accompanies this activity over the course of twenty-three film shots. Through the use of a metronome, Mamoulian organizes all these sounds and shots within a strict tempo and metrical framework in 4/4 or 2/4 time. Judging from the remarks in the Skeleton in January to the

"White Script" in April 1932, the idea of what was then referred to as the "awakening of the Paris street" was present from the start.[14]

If it wasn't the first time that Mamoulian tried something similar, it would also not be the last. The origins for the "Symphony of Noises" in *Love Me Tonight* as Rodgers points out are found in the play *Porgy*.[15] This was the play that marked Mamoulian's historic debut as a Broadway director in 1927. Since the opening of this scene was conceived and written by Mamoulian, it was excluded from the published play, but the full text of the "Symphony of Noises" is conveniently reprinted in Joseph Horowitz's *"On My Way,"* where he places it in act 3, scene 2.[16] Not only does Mamoulian indicate detailed pantomimed stage directions interspersed with snippets of dialogue, he organizes all the activities into eight measures of 4/4 time with each beat accounted for (and in a predetermined tempo).

In *Love Me Tonight*, the human sounds begin with a man striking the cobblestones on the first beat of each measure of a 4/4 meter, this time by a pickax worker who enters on the fifth shot, and the snores of a sleeping man on the third beat starting in the seventh shot and continuing for the next six bars. One measure and one shot later Mamoulian adds the third sound: the sound of a woman with a broom on beats two and four, again duplicating the organization and using the identical sounds of the opening of *Porgy's* act 3, scene 2 (published version act 4, scene 3). Lea Jacobs offers a detailed examination of what we have seen and heard so far, including a useful transcription of every shot and the sounds and rhythms that accompany them, starting with the four opening shots, each synchronized to the tolling of a bell.[17] In the January 8 Skeleton, Mamoulian characterizes the scene as a "work song." This may be a reference to the work songs and field hollers created and sung by African Americans in the American South that presage the blues.

Hannah Lewis offers a useful analysis of how Mamoulian "explores the boundaries between noise and music. . . . In the context of real life, noises may be more naturalistic than musical sounds; but in this cinematic context, noises of everyday life are presented in a more stylized, artificial manner than the song is, making the act of singing seem quite natural by comparison."[18] The "Symphony of Noises" would be exhibit A for a "stylized, artificial manner," that central Mamoulian principle discussed in chapter 1. In Mamoulian's conception, what may have begun as realism soon would evolve into stylization: "I was convinced that sound on the screen should not be constantly shackled by naturalism."[19]

What follows is Jacobs's list and description of the film shots and rhythmic sounds (minus the detailed rhythmic transcription). Note that the shots and musical measures are rarely completely in synch:

- Shot 5: high angle street set; workman enters [2 measures plus 1 beat][20]
- Shot 6: low angle; he wields pick-ax [5 beats]
- Shot 7: high angle, man sleeping on the street [2 beats + 2 measures]
- Shot 8: woman with broom [2 measures + 1 beat]
- Shot 9: chimney tops, smoke emerges [early use of zoom photography] [3 beats + 1 measure + 2 beats]
- Shot 10: window shutter open; alarm clock and baby [2 beats + 2 measures + 1 beat]
- Shot 11: man brings out sawhorse [3 measures]
- Shot 12: school boys on street; metal [2 measures minus 1 eighth-note]
- Shot 13: fruit vendor opens vertical shutter [2 measures + 2 eighth-notes]
- Shot 14: woman on balcony shakes cloth [1 measure minus 2 eighth-notes + 1 measure + 2 eighth-notes]
- Shot 15: exterior shoe store; cobblers bring out benches and begin to strike[21] [1 measure minus 2 eighth-notes + 4 measures]
- Shot 16: man sharpens knives [1 measure]
- Shot 17: street/crowd noise; bike chimes [1 measure minus 1 eighth-note]
- Shot 18: woman beating blanket [1 eighth-note + 1 measure of 2/4 time]
- Shot 19: wagon pushed out of warehouse [2 measures of 2/4 time]
- Shot 20: street with [Maurice's] tailor's shop; taxi horn [first time] [1 measure of 2/4 time + 1 measure of 4/4 time]
- Shot 21: window shutter open; street noise and taxi horn [second time]; [1 measure woman visible in window, she turns inside; gramophone [3 measures of 4/4 time + 1 beat]

Music of the "Street Scene" starts.

- Shot 22: woman on roof hangs out laundry; music gets louder and evokes taxi horn [3 beats + 2 measures of 4/4 time + 2 beats]
- Shot 23: high angle; street (as opening) street noises up [2 beats + 1 measure of 4/4 time]

Other Instrumental Music

"Street Scene," "Maurice Arrives at the Chateau (March Maestoso)," and "The Hunt"

"Street Scene" (3:58–4:43), briefly reprised as "Paris Roofs" (24:29–24:38)

At the precise moment at which the woman places the needle on the gramophone, the sound moves from her apartment to the street exterior and the sound of an external orchestra. The forty-five seconds of "Street Scene" music that follow vividly capture the busy life of a Parisian street, including the horns (or klaxons) blaring above the street traffic. The music consists mainly of the "Street Scene Tune" (Musical Example 2.1), initially heard near the beginning and at the end of the Prelude, now heard as the camera moves from the street to Maurice's room where he first hears the sounds outside his window. At the end of the "Street Scene" Maurice has had enough, closes the window, and complains, "Lovely morning Song of Par*ee*/You are too loud for *me*," which launches "The Song of Paree." During one repetition of the "Street Scene Tune," the scene directions in the copyist's draft score indicate that we should hear the sound of an alarm clock (an instruction observed also in the Conductor's Score and, more softly, at least for an alarm clock, in the film). The copyist's draft indicates that the countermelody above the "Street Scene Tune" will be heard in "The Song of Paree" sung to the words "It has less [faults] than a poor Nanny *Goat's Art*" [rhymes with *Mozart*] in "The Song of Paree."

Rodgers returns to the familiar allusion that he attaches to the horn/klaxon sounds first heard in the final seconds of the "Symphony of Noises," a possible allusion to two works by Gershwin. Fittingly, the first is the three-note authentic Parisian taxi klaxon that emerges from a whole-tone melody early in *An American in Paris* (1928) and eventually is heard another ten times often in close succession all within the first minute of the work. Rodgers's horn motive (Musical Example 3.6a) also shares the rhythm and pitch contours of the "Wintergreen for President" musical campaign slogan in George and Ira Gershwin's hit musical *Of Thee I Sing* (1931), which was still running on Broadway when Rodgers wrote *Love Me Tonight*'s "Street Scene" (Musical Example 3.6a-b).

Musical Example 3.6a-b
a. Klaxons (horns) in "Street Scene"
b. "Wintergreen for President" slogan from *Of Thee I Sing* (George and Ira
Gershwin)

a. Klaxons (horns) in "Street Scene"

b. "Wintergreen for President" slogan from *Of Thee I Sing* (George and Ira Gershwin)

Win-ter-green for Pres-i-dent!

The reason why the klaxon tune constitutes an allusion rather than a quotation of the "Wintergreen for President" motive is that the klaxon motive
outlines an augmented triad, based on the pitches of the whole-tone scale
found in the "Street Scene Tune," while "Wintergreen" outlines a minor triad.
Another difference is that the klaxon stops short of the two final syllables "i-
dent," so that we hear only "Wintergreen for Pres-." Still, the distinctiveness
of the rhythm (four shorts and a long), the number of repetitions (seven in
just over a minute between the end of the "Symphony of Noises" and the end
of the "Street Scene" instrumental), combined with the viewers' potential fa-
miliarity with the "Wintergreen" slogan in late 1931 and throughout 1932,
suggests that Rodgers's horn theme might be considered an likely allusion to
both of these Gershwin themes.

Maurice Arrives at the Chateau ("March Maestoso") (39:36–41:27)

- "Ça Ira," Maurice arrives outside the chateau (39:36–39:52)
- "Minuet" from *Don Giovanni* (Mozart), Maurice enters the hallway of
  the chateau (39:53–40:15)
- "March Maestoso" [Maurice explores the interior of the chateau]
  (40:16–41:27)

Maurice's arrival at the chateau is accompanied by nearly two uninterrupted
minutes of music designated "March Maestoso" ("Majestic March"). The
pantomime begins with two borrowings before continuing with orchestral
underscoring based on "How Are You?," which was most clearly heard in the
"How Are You Interlude" (7:26). The first borrowing is the revolutionary
song "Ça Ira," which accompanies Maurice's arrival outside the chateau

(39:36–39:52). The slow, ceremonial march "Ça Ira" was carefully chosen. According to the *Historical Dictionary of the French Revolution,* the song, which became known in 1790, "was the first popular song of the Revolution" and served as "its revolutionary anthem."[22] The text was by Ladré, a soldier who later became a street singer known only by his surname, and the music composed by the violinist also remembered only by his surname, Bécourt, who played in a Parisian theater orchestra. The idea for this borrowing choice can be traced to the scene when Maurice responds to the angry unpaid shirt maker who expresses his interest in getting a crowd and attacking Gilbert's chateau to get the money he owes: "Let me attack it alone. I'll be a one-man French Revolution. Let me have all the goods the Vicomte ordered. I'll deliver them to the chateau and I'll make him pay!"

By the time Pierre drives Maurice to the chateau in order to receive the long-overdue payments from Gilbert for the unpaid suits, he has met Jeanette in the countryside and fallen in love with her. Eventually he will find her in the chateau, but for the moment he marches to the immense fortress-like front door to the tune of "Ça Ira" like a French revolutionary tearing down the doors of the Bastille. His knocking unanswered, Maurice opens the door and enters the gigantic hallway to the music of the second borrowing, the "Minuet" from the first act finale of Mozart's *Don Giovanni* during the Don's costume party at his palazzo. All the rest of the music heard during Maurice's search for Gilbert is original, composed but probably not arranged by Rodgers.

The music that follows the *Don Giovanni* minuet labeled "March Maestoso" consists of Rodgers's musical transformation of "How Are You?," formerly a big band jazzy refrain, now a march. The Conductor's Score describes a number of Maurice's actions, all of which are perfectly synchronized musically.[23] When Maurice takes a step the music takes a step. When he goes faster the music goes faster, and when he stops abruptly the music follows suit. Here are all the directions in the order they appear: "Must follow footsteps," "puts foot down," "He looks in door to right," "take[s] step," "c.u. [close up] door way," "change angle," "near door in back," "walking," "near steps," "making steps," "2x stop for action," "start with Chev[alier] walks," "on landing," "starts upstairs again," "little faster," "going up stairway," "faster," "going up," "faster," "going up," "last stairway," "How are you?," "step with Chev[alier] on top of stairway." As originally filmed, at the end of his journey Chevalier finds himself in Jeanette's bedroom where the two sing "Letter Song" ("The Man for Me"). As discussed in previous chapters, the song was cut. Instead, Maurice simply descends the stairs and "looks thru the doorway" at the residents as the music plays "Hail! Hail! The Gang's All Here" from Gilbert and Sullivan's *The Pirates of Penzance* composed in 1879. And indeed the gang (but not yet Jeanette) is all there.

The practice of synchronizing every movement with matching music is widely referred to as "Mickey Mousing." The label used to be a high compliment, for example when Billy says to his friend Reno in Cole Porter's song "You're the Top" from *Anything Goes* two years after *Love Me Tonight,* "You're Mickey Mouse," a reference to Mickey as a beloved character rather than the mimicking process of Mickey Mousing. In ensuing decades, the compliment evolved into an insult, and an innovative mannerist exaggeration became a ludicrously obvious mannerism associated with cartoons. The following passage in a contemporary text on film music is a case in point: "Such mimicking of movement and sound is quite common in cartoons. Since films are supposed to be more realistic, composers tend to be careful not to match the music too closely to the action. When the music is too obvious—for example accenting every step of someone walking—it is appropriately termed Mickey Mousing."[24] In discussing the contemporaneous *King Kong* (1933), the author of this quote, Roger Hickman, notes that "such obvious mimicking of a physical movement (Mickey Mousing) is now considered a weakness in film music."[25] But as we are by now getting to know Mamoulian, we are learning that he couldn't care less about realism. Instead, his often-stated vision of a film called for stylization, an approach readily observed in the synchronized rhythms of the Parisian workers as they begin their morning "Symphony of Noises" and will again be observed in "The Hunt." By this definition, Mamoulian might argue that Maurice's exploration of the chateau is actually further evidence of stylization over realism.

"The Hunt" (52:20–57:14)

As he would do in *On Your Toes* four years later, once in each act, Rodgers composed a ballet for *Love Me Tonight.* Since it involved live-action dancing animals instead of people, he referred to it as his "zoological ballet": "One sequence I was particularly proud of was the scoring for the deer hunt.[26] In it I had to create two contrasting and intercutting themes, one—on the brass—for the pursuing dogs and horses, the other—on the strings—for the frightened deer." As Rodgers notes, Mamoulian staged the entire sequence as if were a "zoological ballet."[27] The extant nine-page "handwritten score" manuscript on piano-vocal score paper, which is not in Rodgers's hand, uses the vocal line for additional instrumental parts. This allowed for a number of instrumental indications. Both the handwritten score and the Conductor's Score also provide titles, "Pastorale," "The Hunt," and "La Sortie de L'eau," and detail the cutting back and forth between the deer and the dogs conceived by Rodgers by labeling each appearance.[28] Although Rodgers claims in his autobiography that he was responsible for the scoring of the deer hunt, the extent to which he was the "auteur" of these scoring details is not clear from the surviving manuscript evidence.

"The Hunt" begins with an introduction featuring horns and trumpet in a 6/8 "hunting style" with the horns emphasizing thirds and sixths but ending all the phrases on open fifths, the quintessential Romantic horn interval. The result is music that sounds quite like any number of hunting choruses that frequent early German Romantic opera. At the "Pastorale," viewers catch their first glimpse of the prey, a grazing deer ("diss[olve] to Deer"), which Rodgers indicated should be scored for flute. Since the deer hasn't sensed danger yet, its eighth-note rhythm is slower and non-pizzicato and ends with a short florid cadenza consisting of eight thirty-second notes.

Once the dogs find the scent, the music increases to a rapid tempo, and the rest of the hunt consists of rapidly alternating musical and visual depictions of the dogs (the horses aren't expressly identified) and the deer. As Rodgers notes, the barking dogs are given to the brass with trumpet fanfares, with open fourths and fifths assigned to the horns. The meter is 6/8 time. At every "cut to deer," the meter shifts to 2/4 time with pizzicato violins and the xylophone depicting the deer while the horns and trombone play a single muted pitch. By the end of the hunt both the deer and the dogs have been heard no fewer than seven times. The cuts are also swift, with only three to seven seconds separating them.

To depict the deer component of the ballet Rodgers incorporates the precise rhythm and alludes to (and briefly quotes) the opening of a famous ballet movement originally designed for human dancers. The source is the "Pizzicato" from *Sylvia* (1876) by Leo Delibes (see Musical Example 3.7a-b).

The rhythm of Rodgers's deer shown in Example 3.7a is the same as the Delibes (Example 3.7b). The second part of Rodgers's deer music (not shown) displays the successive perfect fourths in the melody also found in Delibes's ballet. What better way to capture the balletic grace of a deer in a

Musical Example 3.7a-b
a. "Deer Theme" from "The Hunt" ("Quassi [*sic*] Fairy") (52:57)
b. "Pizzicato" movement from *Sylvia* by Leo Delibes (beginning)

"zoological ballet" than to assign it a passage that suggests a famous human ballet?[29]

The hunt (and its music) is interrupted when Jeanette finds Maurice in a hunting lodge feeding the prey, much to her disapproval. Jeanette accuses Maurice of not being a gentleman (because he doesn't know the rules of the hunt). Maurice counters by accusing Jeanette of not being a woman: "You know too much about hunting, etiquette, tradition. You know nothing about style." The Duke arrives, interrupting the quarreling lovers to inquire what's going on. Maurice explains that the poor tired deer is asleep and shouldn't be disturbed. Although the Duke finds this request ridiculous, he honors it, and the First Aunt and Gilbert follow the Duke's instruction to "go back quickly and quietly, on tiptoes."

The word "tiptoes" is the cue for the Duke and the others to depart on their horses in a slow motion variation of the opening hunting music, another example of Mamoulian's stylization in action. Their speaking and laughing is underscored and eventually dissolves into a conversation with the Count to whom the Duke laughingly reports that the "Baron and the deer made friends, and called the whole thing off." The Count, who has spent the hunt searching for evidence concerning Maurice's questionable nobility, reports that even though he's "been through the better class illegitimates," he hasn't been able to locate any nobility with the name Courtelin (Maurice's assumed surname). Gilbert, who knows Maurice's identity, chimes in that the name Baron Courtelin is "a mere nom de Pullman." Viewers too young to remember the Pullman sleeping cars that disappeared from American trains in the 1960s after 100 years of common use may be excused if they miss Gilbert's silly play on "nom de plume."

Delicious, the first film with a complete score by George and Ira Gershwin, opened on December 27, 1931, one day after *Of Thee I Sing* on Broadway, both events less than one month before the first known treatments and songs for *Love Me Tonight*. Perhaps *Delicious*'s most atypical feature was the inclusion of two substantial instrumental numbers composed by George, a sung dream sequence called "Welcome to the Melting Pot" and a "New York Rhapsody," the latter forming the basis of Gershwin's Second Rhapsody for piano and orchestra. A few years later when George and Ira returned to Hollywood, George composed some of the instrumental music for his second film with Ira, *Shall We Dance* (1937). The additional orchestral music included some two-piano music to accompany the "French Ballet Class" and "Dance of the Waves" at the beginning of the film and most famously the "Walking the Dog" segment during which Fred Astaire and Ginger Rogers walk their respective dogs along the deck of a ship.[30] For George and Ira's third film, *Damsel in Distress* (starring Astaire and Joan Fontaine), released in November several months after Gershwin died in early July 1937, Gershwin even scored the main tunes, which like those in *Love Me Tonight*, were composed by George with lyrics by his brother Ira before the screenplay was written.[31]

What Rodgers was asked to do was therefore not unprecedented, but it would be considered unusual in its time and might still spark notice to this day. Most composers then and now are not asked to contribute anything beyond the songs, nor could most songsmiths successfully take on this added compositional burden if they were asked. But Mamoulian "insisted" that Rodgers could contribute "all the background music, not simply the music for the songs." It would be hoped that the instrumental music discussed in this chapter demonstrates that Rodgers rose to the occasion and successfully created a soundtrack that could support Mamoulian's vision.

Love Me Tonight was the beginning of a remarkably creative partnership between Rodgers and Mamoulian. Having made Hollywood history in 1932, Rodgers and Mamoulian would meet again to make Broadway history eleven years later, this time with Oscar Hammerstein, first with *Oklahoma!* in 1943 and then with *Carousel* in 1945.

4

Sex and Censorship

"A Jewish-owned business selling Roman Catholic theology to
Protestant America."

Unattributed but widely quoted description of
the Production Code

Introduction

When Paramount Pictures released *Love Me Tonight* on August 1932, various state censorship boards requested the removal of one passage or another from the prints shown in their particular fiefdoms. Not one of these states, Canadian provinces, or anyone on the continent of Australia for that matter complained about the appropriateness of the gossamer nightgown Myrna Loy wore when she awakened the morning after Maurice's. arrival and took her turn with fellow chateau residents for a reprised chorus of "Mimi." Seventeen years later, censorship czar Joseph I. Breen singled out Loy's outfit as one of three expurgations required in order for Paramount to obtain permission from the Production Code Administration (PCA), better known as the Production Code, the Hays Code, or simply the Code, for a restricted release.[1] Breen's directive was to the point: "Delete the scene of Myrna Loy in the transparent nightgown."[2] As a consequence of Breen's decision, Loy's outfit and her fifteen seconds of musical fame witnessed in 1932 were stricken from the film record when the film was rereleased in 1949.

Both Loy's nightgown and vocal excerpt remained missing when *Love Me Tonight* was eventually released on VHS and DVD formats in 2003. The reason for their continued absence was the same as it was in 1949: in response to the PCA, Paramount destroyed the master camera negatives, and the destruction was irreversible. All that survives is a photograph shown in Figure 4.1 that was cut from the negative prior to the reissue.[3]

In her memoir, Loy attributed her excision from the film to the visibility of her navel.[4] The photograph contradicts this memory. While it reveals a

Love Me Tonight. Geoffrey Block, Oxford University Press. © Oxford University Press 2024.
DOI: 10.1093/9780197566220.003.0004

Figure 4.1 Myrna Loy in her controversial nightgown.

low-cut negligée made with a diaphanous fabric that reveals her legs, Loy's navel is not in evidence, at least not to the naked eye.

In 1932, the Studio Relations Committee (SRC), as the Pre-Code censorship office was called, had monitored and censored film content on behalf of the Motion Picture Producers and Distributors of America (MPPDA) for only two years.[5] The good news for *Love Me Tonight* is that the Code was not rigorously enforced until two years later in 1934 when the relentless PCA enforcer Breen, who replaced the SRC's more congenial Colonel Jason S. Joy that summer, started to keep films that did not earn a certificate for good behavior out of theatrical distribution nationwide, including several films directed by Mamoulian. In the case of *Love Me Tonight*, Breen's directive required two other deletions (to be discussed later) in addition to the permanent removal of Loy's nightgown, which resulted in the removal of her vocal chorus from the film.

This chapter will begin by exploring how the Association of Motion Picture Producers (AMPP), the West Coast division of the MPPDA, addressed censorship issues related to *Love Me Tonight* during the film's production and initial release in 1932 under the auspices of the SRC. This is the period generally known as the Pre-Code era (1930–1934).[6] The second part of the story concerns the rerelease of *Love Me Tonight* in 1949 under Breen's PCA (1934–1968). Although state censorship boards made numerous demands for deletions to *Love Me Tonight* upon its initial release, the SRC made only one small official deletion (despite expressing some concerns on a number of possible censorship issues). The decision to delete the song "The Man for Me" belonged solely to Mamoulian, not to any objections raised by the SRC.

Perhaps more significant than what was questioned or censored was what made it *past* the SRC in 1932 and even the PCA in 1949. *Love Me Tonight* clearly dodged the censors' bullets by being made in the Pre-Code era. Memos written by Breen in 1936 and 1937 strongly suggest that had *Love Me Tonight* been originally created in 1934 rather than two years earlier, it is likely that the fundamental nature and quantity of necessary revisions required would have prohibited its release. But the damage was done. Even though viewers were able to see most of the film after waiting seventeen years, no one got to see *Love Me Tonight* from 1932 to 1949. This degree of neglect is a lot for a classic film to bear (see Table 4.1 at the end of the chapter).[7]

Issues related to censorship can be observed through numerous extant inter-office memos from 1932, mainly between Colonel Joy, the director of the SRC from 1926 to 1932 (or his assistant Lamar Trotti), and Paramount's associate producer and managing director of production B. P. Schulberg, also from 1926 to 1932.[8] In contrast to his successor, Joy fits Mark A. Vieira's succinct description of an executive who "would not attack a film because it dealt with adult issues," a script reader who "found a way to express its complex morality without shocking anyone," and was in general "even-tempered, deliberate, thoughtful."[9] Although Joy wanted films to punish characters who were unrepentant in their immorality, in many cases he "acted more as advocate than censor" and "devoted much time to protecting serious but controversial pictures from abusive cuts by local, state, and foreign censor boards."[10] In connection with *Love Me Tonight,* which he clearly considered a worthy film, Joy seemed to view his role as someone who could provide friendly advice, which, if taken, would avoid the state censorship problems most likely to arise. This chapter will show that Joy was mostly prescient in his predictions.

Censorship and the Song Lyrics (January to April 1932)

While the script was in development from January to March 1932, Rodgers and Hart wrote the songs. During the process of their completion the first phase of the censorship review began when Jesse L. Lasky Jr. (son of Paramount co-founder Jesse L. Lasky Sr.) forwarded the first lyrics to Joy, who in turn directed his endorsements and suggestions to Schulberg. After receiving the first lyric, "Isn't It Romantic?," on January 11, Joy replied to Schulberg that he judged the lyric "satisfactory from the standpoint of the Code and contains nothing reasonably censorable." In his January 28 response to Schulberg regarding the next lyric received, "The Song of Paree," Joy expressed the SRC's position that the expression "thank God" in the first stanza "should not be used in this connection." [11] In the single instance of compliance with a lyric suggestion from the SRC, Hart changed "Thank God it's no Viennese waltz" to "But at least it's no Viennese waltz." Although the words "Thank God" remain in the Conductor's Score, the film and published *Complete Lyrics of Lorenz Hart* used the censored version.[12] In his next letter to Joy, dated February 19, which accompanied the lyrics to "The Man for Me" and "The Son-of-a-Gun Is Nothing but a Tailor," Lasky defended the latter title and argued for its importance as "the key line as well as the title of the song," a line that in Lasky's view "certainly carries no immoral significance." Three days later Joy agreed and found both lyrics "satisfactory etc."

In contrast, when it came to the next pair of lyrics, "A Woman Needs Something Like That" and "Love Me Tonight," received respectively on March 7 and 9, Joy shared some qualms. In his response to "A Woman" on March 8, although he didn't think "many people" would find its "amusing" lyrics "offensive," Joy felt the "thought itself" ventured "a little too far in innuendo." In the end, while Joy was concerned that a film he regarded as "delightful and clever" might be placed in jeopardy "by going too far beyond the line between the risqué into the suggestive," he offered no specific remedies. Joy was right to be worried about "A Woman Needs Something Like That" since portions of this song would be singled out by a number of state censorship boards later in 1932. In 1949 it would become the second of the three deletions that Breen demanded (the first was the removal of Loy and her outfit in the "Mimi" reprise). But upon its initial release, despite Joy's reservations, apart from the individual state boards who objected to various lyrics in the song, "A Woman" remained unchanged and unexpurgated.

Responding on March 12 to the lyrics of the title song ("Love Me Tonight") Joy noted that "the only line which seems questionable at all is: 'Must we sleep tonight all alone?'" Even while voicing this concern, the characteristically open-minded Joy realized that "much will depend on the relationship of the song to the play." In keeping with the give and take of Joy's exchanges with Lasky and Schulberg, Lasky proposed an alternative rhyming line, "let's drink deep tonight all alone." This time Hart's original line (from the verse of the song) was allowed to remain and can be seen in the *Complete Lyrics*, but since the original film and the 1949 rerelease removed the verse entirely, the lyric "Must we sleep tonight all alone?" was no longer an issue.

While the Pre-Production Code files include the letter from March 19 in which Lasky sent the lyrics to "Mimi," they lack a response from Joy. Consequently, there is no record of any requests to change a lyric to this song, and in any event they weren't altered. On April 4, Lasky sent a second request to Joy (the first is not included in the files) inquiring whether "there should be any censorable lines" in "The Poor Apache," "as the picture is going into production" that week.[13] Joy responded positively to Schulberg the next day affirming that the SRC had "no further suggestions to make."

In this same letter, Joy returned to the lyrics of "A Woman Needs Something Like That," which he and others usually identified as "the doctor's song": "There is still question in our minds about the doctor's song. Perhaps you are right in thinking it will be less questionable when it is sung. At least I share with you the hope that this will be true." Several weeks later on April 19 Trotti brought up "the doctor's song" again in his response to the White Script: "The Doctor's song is still dubious, although as we said before perhaps it will be far less so when it is recorded." In the same letter, Trotti also suggests the removal of the words "for France," when the soldiers sing "we would rather sing than fight for France" in "Isn't It Romantic?" as an offence against "national feelings," a censorship issue (to be defined shortly). When the film was released, Paramount would disregard this suggestion as well.

Trotti's letter is the final reference to song lyrics prior to the completion of the shooting script and the release of the film in August. With the exception of "Lover," the record confirms that all the songs were submitted to and approved by the SRC. The verdict of all this discussion clearly ended up in favor of the defense. Aside from removing the words "thank God" in "The Song of Paree," Hart had received permission to use *all* of his original lyrics in the original release of *Love Me Tonight*, although they ended up not using the verse to "Love Me Tonight."

Censorship and the Screenplay (March, April, and August 1932)

Two days after Lasky sent Joy the Buff Script on March 26 Joy responded with alacrity that he had read it "with great amusement" and found it "to contain elements which will make it satisfactory under the Code."[14] Nevertheless, repeating his comments of March 7 verbatim, Joy yet again brought up the doctor's song, "the only thing" in the script he significantly questioned from a "censorship point of view." A smaller "possible worry," "the light references to Bastile [*sic*] Day," led Joy to suggest their removal so as to not offend any current French Royalists who might "take exception to them." Joy concluded the letter with the promise to think about this potential issue and then get back to Schulberg. The next day, Joy followed through on his promise and wrote to Schulberg with the assurance that he needn't worry about the French Royalists after all.

In this March 29 missive Joy also offered two new suggestions. The first was to "safeguard yourself against criticism by refraining from addressing the Princess as 'Your Highness,'" so as to not imply royal blood. In the second suggestion, Joy asked Paramount to consider omitting "the scenes of the princess striking a servant with her riding whip," an action to which Royalists and Republicans alike would surely object.[15] In response to Joy's modest suggestions, Mamoulian and his screenwriters removed a literal reference to Bastille Day (i.e., "descriptions of the preparations for celebrating the 14th of July") and the whipping of servants but continued to allow Princess Jeanette to be addressed as royalty.[16] Joy's sensitivity to the sensibilities of Royalists and Republicans is in keeping with the tenth item of the "Particular Applications" of the Code, "National Feelings": "*The history*, institutions, prominent people and citizenry of all nations shall be represented fairly."[17] The Code wasn't only about sex.

In addition to bringing up the above concerns in his response to the White Script, Trotti found one short scene unsatisfactory under the Code. This was the scene "where Gilbert [Charles Ruggles]—wearing only shorts, undershirt and shoes—is caught in a room with a woman who is reclining on a bed." Curiously, Trotti's "chief objection" was that *Gilbert* was undressed, and although it is clear from the script when the woman's husband discovers Gilbert in the woman's boudoir that she is married, Trotti refrains from calling attention to this seemingly crucial fact. Trotti, who understood that the bedroom scene merged into the following scene in which Gilbert finds himself running in his underwear in an "Across-Paris Run" (an important element in the plot), was nonetheless confident they could devise "some less questionable situation."

Paramount decided instead to remove the questionable bedroom scene entirely, although they kept Gilbert in his underwear and retained the dialogue that explains how he ended up running in the street underdressed. Aside from the removal of "The Man for Me," which was voluntary, the bedroom scene with Gilbert in his underwear and a married woman confronting her cuckolded husband, was the only excision either suggested or executed. Readers may recall from the end of chapter 1 how Trotti, despite his lingering reservations about the doctor's song, concluded his remarks to Lasky with the highest compliment a censor could safely make to a movie studio executive: "May I add that in general this is one of the most delightful scripts I have ever read."[18]

On August 8, 1932, ten days before the film's official New York release, Joy, Trotti, and SRC reviewers John V. Wilson and James B. Fisher noted that they had seen "the new Chevalier picture, LOVE ME TONIGHT." This memo is the first of several occasions to note that nearly everyone, including reviewers (as we will see in chapter 5) seemed to think of the film primarily as a vehicle for Chevalier, the French star. Anticipating potential problems with the state censorship boards, Joy offered advice to Paramount supervisor Harold Hurley on how they might address them prior to the film's official release. Still at the top of Joy's concerns was the "Doctor's Song" ("A Woman Needs Something Like That"). Joy's second warning related to Gilbert's attempt to explain why he joined the marathon runners in his shorts and undershirt (a problem) to escape the irate husband who suddenly returned to find his wife in bed with another man (apparently not a problem).

Joy's third and most pressing warning (not a directive) relates to the conversation about the Virgin's Spring, "especially when Myrna Loy [Valentine] tells Chevalier she will show it to him in private if there is a moon, and [Charles] Butterworth's [Count Savignac's] remark: I didn't know there was one in the neighborhood." Speaking for the SRC, Joy concludes his prescient list of possible censorship problems with praise and optimism for the latest film of the popular Frenchman: "This seems to all of us one of the best of the Chevalier pictures. It ought to be a great success."

On August 11 Joy wrote to James B. Fitzgerald of the Washington Film Board of Trade, elaborating on the points he made to Hurley two days earlier. He opens the letter praising the "Chevalier picture" as "one of the best that he has ever done." He then repeats his worry that the censors will object to "the talk about the 'virgin springs' [virgin's spring]" and encourages the studio to remove the conversation "since it has no story significance." In contrast to his letter to Hurley, however, Joy refrains from sharing any concern about the propriety of Gilbert's explanation of how he lost his pants.

Joy also returns to the red flags he noted earlier regarding "A Woman Needs Something Like That." This time he mentions a particular lyric that encompasses the song's title: "Bells need tinkling, flowers need sprinkling, and a woman needs something like that." Since he personally finds these lyrics amusing and inoffensive, he hopes the censors will let Paramount keep them, just as he hopes the studio "won't lose the last line of the Apache song where Chevalier says: 'Nuts to you.'" After suggesting the possibility of inviting censors to join live theater audiences to test the waters (a plan rejected without comment by Paramount), Joy concludes this letter as positively as his previous letter to Hurley: "I'm sure audiences are going to love it and will get no sense of suggestiveness out of the songs." The same day, Fisher filed the following highly laudatory SRC staff report: "A charming and amusing picture thoroughly enjoyable from start to finish. The lyrics are splendid and the director has employed a most original style in putting them across. The cast is superb and every role boasts a distinguished performance."[19]

Censorship and the Finished Film (August 1932)

Both during the creation of the film and after it was made, Colonel Joy and his assistants worked to interpret and enforce the 1930–1934 version of the Code and asked Paramount to remove suggestive passages of dialogue and some lyrics considered inappropriate. Perhaps surprisingly, virtually none of the suggestions offered by the Code keepers were followed in the finished film. On the other hand, in selected state censorship boards, some Canadian provinces, and Australia, exhibitors demanded the removal of material considered offensive before copies of the film were released in those areas. The memos show precisely what was considered objectionable and offer specific examples of what should be done about it. For example, Massachusetts, a state with only a single problem with a Hart lyric in "The Poor Apache," noted that "these eliminations are required only for Sunday showing."

Overall, the exchanges between Paramount and the SRC from January to August 1932 exerted a minimal direct impact on the finished film released on August 18. As previously noted, Joy's suggestions for the lyrics led to a single change, the removal of two words, "thank God," from "The Song of Paree." All the other warnings fell on deaf ears. Concerning the screenplay, Paramount may have deleted an explicit reference to Bastille Day and the whipping of a servant, but it retained the Revolutionary trope of storming the chateau. And for the record, in the final film viewers can still hear Doctor Armand de Pontignac address Princess Jeanette as "Your Highness." The only requested elimination observed in the completed film in 1932 was the removal of the scene when a husband returns unexpectedly to find his wife and Gilbert in the same bedroom.

Still, when it comes to Joy's central concern, the state (and Canadian) censorship boards, Joy's fears were amply realized. We don't hear too much about these regional censorship boards in the Breen era (1934–54) because the rigorous oversight of scripts and the final films offered under the PCA starting in July 1934 made them far less necessary, if not obsolete. In the Pre-Code era under the SRC from 1930 to mid-1934, the censorship boards came to the rescue when the SRC either would not, or could not, enforce their moral will upon the studios. In the case of *Love Me Tonight,* Joy clearly and correctly saw the potential for problems with the censorship boards, but since he didn't find the *potentially* problematic dialogue in "A Woman Needs Something Like That" personally repugnant, he let the individual boards decide what they wanted to censor.

Most of the state-by-state censorship demands to remove a lyric or a few lines, or in three instances, a frame or two, are unique to a particular board. For example, the board in Ontario, Canada, removed the two times the Count remarked that he fell on his flute. Indeed, a high percentage of the total requested eliminations of both lyrics and dialogue in 1932 came from the censorship office in Ontario. On the other hand, as Joy suspected, several boards requested the removal of all or a portion of the "doctor's song" ("A Woman Needs Something Like That"), Gilbert's explanation of why he is running in a street foot race in his shorts and undershirt, and varying amounts of dialogue about the "Virgin's Spring." With the significant exception of the Ontario board with its numerous eliminations, the demands of most boards were relatively modest. Three states and Quebec had no problems with anything at all and simply stamped "approved without eliminations" (see Table 4.1 at the end of the chapter).

The boards acquired their initial authority as a response to a Supreme Court case from 1915, *Mutual Film Corporation v. Industrial Commission of Ohio*, which concluded that in contrast to the press, which was protected by the First Amendment, movies were "a business, pure and simple, originated and conducted for profit."[20] Although the film industry thought the censorship boards would be preferable to the kind of federal regulation of labeling recently instituted by the Food and Drug Administration (which first acquired that name in 1930), proliferating state censorship boards "screened, cut, and certified every frame of celluloid projected within local borders, tormenting motion picture distributors with an obstacle course whose hurdles stretched from state to state, city to city. . . . Worse, filmmakers had to pay for the trouble."[21] Vieira notes that "in 1928 the New York Board cut four thousand scenes from six hundred films" and the Chicago Board another six thousand scenes (to take just two examples) and that "censor boards were costing the industry $3.5 million a year in review fees, salaries, and mutilated prints."[22]

Leonard J. Leff and Jerold L. Simmons succinctly summarized the problem: "The Code concerned morals; the *adoption* of the Code concerned money."[23] In 1934, soon after Catholic leaders successfully persuaded twenty million practitioners to boycott *all* films, the major film studios, largely managed by Jews, concluded that managing morality was also good for business. This was the dynamic that led to the epigraph placed at the head of this chapter regarding the essence of the Production Code, "A Jewish-owned business selling Roman Catholic theology to Protestant America."[24] The situation was analogous to contemporary discussions of self-regulation by the big internet companies as an alternative (for the moment) to effective governmental regulations.

Unlike the SRC, the PCA had the power to review every script and every finished film. This was in sharp contrast to 1929, one year before the

Pre-Code era began, when Joy received only 20 percent of the screenplays and more than 60 percent of industry revenue came from states that had censor boards.[25] As a result of increased scrutiny at the top in the PCA era, where Breen and his staff exercised their new-found authority to review all new film scripts, state censor boards soon began to decline in importance. Thomas Doherty summarizes the effect of this dramatic structural change: "Once a chronic migraine, the censorship boards receded into a low-level head-ache."[26] The PCA centralized the censorship process and certificated each finished film, ensuring that a censored film could not be shown nationally. This made the state boards less relevant and consequently less powerful.

The Production Code versus *Love Me Tonight* (1934–1949)

In addition to reviewing every script, Breen reviewed numerous requests to rerelease potentially popular films originally issued in the Pre-Code era such as *Love Me Tonight*. In order to organize his response to the studio and the public's desire for these rereleases, Breen divided the Pre-Code films into three categories: "In Class I were those withdrawn immediately, never to be released. Class II included those pictures that would be allowed to complete extant contracts, then be permanently withdrawn; Class III comprised those that would be withdrawn, reedited to conform to the Code, then presented to the Production Code Administration."

Perhaps as expected, Breen placed Mae West's *She Done Him Wrong* and *I'm No Angel* in Class I, although the practical-minded MPPDA Chairman Will H. Hays was amenable to rereleasing both.[27] More controversially, Breen rejected Paramount's requests to rerelease Ernst Lubitsch's critically acclaimed *Trouble in Paradise* and lesser-known *Design for Living,* Joseph von Sternberg's *The Blue Angel,* and Mamoulian's *Song of Songs.* The only silver lining to the ignominious fate of Breen's Class I films was that, since they were rejected outright, their original negatives were spared the perma-nent destruction delivered by the censor's knife. Ironically, it was only be-cause they were beneath Breen's contempt that Class I films were spared the dire fate bestowed on Class III films, including *Love Me Tonight,* shortly be-fore its rerelease in 1949.

On September 24, 1936, thirteen years prior to its eventual rerelease but only four years after its initial release, Vincent Hart, an "association counsel" working in the PCA's New York office, called to Breen's attention an inquiry concerning the possibility of screening *Love Me Tonight* and ten other Pre-Code films at a large revival house on Saturday nights.[28] Four days later (September 28) Breen pledged his allegiance to the Code's first General Principle that "no picture shall be produced which will lower the moral standards of those who see it."[29] Since he didn't think these pictures adhered to this principle, Breen wrote back that "most of these pictures are bad, and cannot be approved by us."

The following day (September 29) Breen's assistant Islin Auster prepared a memo for Hart with brief annotations on the eleven films under consideration (three by Paramount including *Love Me Tonight*, six by MGM, and one each by Universal and Warner Bros.). The directive on two films was "suggest withdrawal or rejection," two were assigned a "doubtful" assessment and a request for further review, and another two were labeled as "questionable" with requests for further review. Only four films were given the "OK" without further comment. *Love Me Tonight* received a unique assessment that left it relatively unscathed: "Refer to red penciled censor cuts. Acceptable with deletions."

On October 2 Breen expressed his objections to Hays concerning the plan of a Washington, DC, exhibitor who sought the rerelease of these eleven pictures, including *Love Me Tonight*, on the grounds that they "gave us a good deal of trouble at the time they were released, and whose reissue at this time might spell disaster." On January 20, 1937, Breen rejected the application to reissue *Love Me Tonight* and a second film, *Guilty as Hell*.[30] Breen based his objections to *Love Me Tonight* on both the dialogue and the lyrics: "After an inspection of the files and records in connection with this picture, we would suggest that you withdraw your application, as it apparently contains a great deal of suggestive dialogue. Some of the lyrics seem to be particularly offensive in this respect, and it would seem, from a cursory inspection, that any attempt to re-edit it would ruin the picture."[31]

The next *Love Me Tonight* item in the Production Code Administration files is a telegram sent on July 17, 1940, from Breen to MPPDA secretary Carl E. Milliken in New York's PCA office, inquiring whether *Love Me Tonight* had been approved for a reissue certificate. Milliken responded by telegram the next day informing Breen that not only had the PCA not approved the film for reissue but that the request was for the limited release of a shorter version rather than a general release of the full-length version. Writing in telegraph shorthand, Milliken concluded that "approval of title somewhat doubtful in view of recent rejection of similar titles including 'I Am Yours for Tonight,' 'Tonight I Am Yours' and 'Tonight We Love.'" A week later (on July 25) Breen sent a certificate of limited approval for *Love Me Tonight* to Paramount's censorship liaison Luigi Luraschi for "**exact copies** of the picture, hereby approved."

The Production Code and the 1949 Rerelease

Despite getting a green light from the PCA in 1940 for a short version designed for limited release, *Love Me Tonight* was not released. For nearly a decade *Love Me Tonight*'s paper trail in the Production Files of the Margaret Herrick Library, one that has served us so faithfully since 1932, would vanish without a trace. Finally, on September 26, 1949, PCA's Geoffrey Shurlock composed a short but informative "Memo for the Files."[32] From this memo we learn that the "shorter version" mentioned by Milliken and approved in 1940 was only a shadow of the 1932 future classic, "a cut-down four-reel version of the original film" (which had ten reels). Shurlock explains what happened: "As a matter of record, after attempting to sell it and failing, the project was abandoned."[33]

Also on September 26, Breen wrote to Luraschi informing him that the PCA had reviewed *Love Me Tonight* four days earlier on September 22 and was prepared to approve the film for release "merely in a few selected art theaters and other theaters of that restricted type." Since the film would be restricted, Breen mandated only three deletions. Here they are, quoted verbatim:

1. Delete both references (in two separate short scenes) to the "virgin springs [virgin's spring]."
2. Delete the Doctor's song, "A Woman Needs Something Like That."
3. Delete the scene of Myrna Loy in the transparent nightgown.

Breen concludes his directive by pointing out that should Paramount later wish to place the picture in general release, "it will be necessary for us to re-review it, and make some further deletions." On October 20 Luraschi assured Breen that Paramount deleted everything the PCA had asked for, and on October 25 Breen sealed the deal and repeated the conditions of the film's "limited reissue in restricted type of theaters."[34] Based on these deletions the film would become the version of *Love Me Tonight* shown in theaters,

television, and on YouTube ever since, including the version released simultaneously on VHS and DVD in 2003.

As might be expected, Breen's first two mandated deletions contained the
passages of dialogue and song lyrics that most concerned Joy in 1932. But
neither Joy nor any of the state censors expressed concern for the nightgown
that revealed the legs (but not the navel) underneath Loy's translucent nightgown during her fifteen seconds of infamy. Breen's directive on Loy's outfit
should not come as a surprise. Even in Shurlock's more benign regime after
Breen's retirement in 1954, the PCA censor reports are full of suggestions
on how to reduce the potential seductiveness of clothing worn by female
characters in a film. To take one example to stand for many, production files
housed in the Josh Logan Collection of the Library of Congress confirm that
Shurlock requested the producers at Twentieth Century-Fox to make sure
Nellie Forbush's robe "not be suggestively short" on the screen when viewers
watched Mitzi Gaynor perform this role in the 1958 film version of *South
Pacific*.[35]

The two short scenes in *Love Me Tonight* that refer to the Virgin's Spring
follow in close succession sandwiched by a brief exchange when Valentine and
Maurice first meet in the chateau. At the first conversation about the Virgin's
Spring between Valentine, the Count, and Gilbert prior to Maurice's arrival,
Valentine offers to show the men the spring. In response, Gilbert asks whether
she is referring to a new dance, and the Count quips, "I didn't know there
was one in the neighborhood," a line that was stricken when the film played
in Ontario and Australia in 1932. In all the states, following this observation,
Valentine, Gilbert, and the Count leave together arm in arm to see the spring.

The second conversation about the Virgin's Spring takes place soon after
Valentine and Maurice meet. Immediately attracted to the tailor, Valentine
expresses her regret that Maurice missed the tour and offers to show it to him
privately. Repeating Gilbert's response, Maurice asks whether she's referring
to a new dance. It's a silly question whose origins might be traced to the pro-
liferation of trendy dances of the day with ridiculous titles. The exchange between Valentine and Maurice was eliminated in Ohio and British Columbia,
but like the first conversation about the spring it was retained in the original
1932 release. Following this second conversation, Valentine asks if Maurice
is married and when he says he is not Valentine responds without hesitation
that she will "be right down." Valentine's eager reply was removed only in
Ohio in 1932 and thankfully allowed to remain in 1949 when the film was
approved "for limited reissue in restricted types of theaters."

Discussions of virgins and the state of virginity, if not a virgin's spring, became a major source of controversy a few years later in a film directed by Otto Preminger, *The Moon Is Blue* (1953). Preminger's film, which arrived near the end of Breen's reign, became a major test case that challenged the authority of the Code. Only one year earlier Preminger had directed *The Miracle*, the film that paved the way for the Supreme Court to reverse the 1915 decision that rejected a film's claim to protection under the First Amendment. In the popular literature fed by Preminger's public relations offensive, the keepers of the Code objected to the frequent use of words such as "virgin" and "seduce." This is an oversimplification. The reason Breen denied certification to *The Moon Is Blue* was not simply for speaking these words but the film's "unacceptably light attitude toward seduction, illicit sex, chastity and virginity."[36] When the PCA refused to give *Moon* the Seal of Approval, several theater chains decided to book the film anyway. It took two years, but eventually the US Supreme Court overturned the ban issued by the Supreme Court of Kansas. In assessing the significance of this war between the film industry and its regulators, Leff and Simmons concluded that "*The Moon Is Blue* sounded the death rattle of the [Catholic] Legion of Decency and the Production Code."[37]

In his January 20, 1937, memo Breen accuses *Love Me Tonight* of containing "a great deal of suggestive dialogue" and some "particularly offensive" lyrics. Interestingly, his objection to *Love Me Tonight* was not dissimilar to his objections to *The Moon Is Blue* twenty years later. Even though there is no consummated sex in either film, both films talk a lot about sex in ways that might be construed to violate "the sanctity of the institution of marriage" and present illicit sex "attractively" (Production Code, Particular Applications, II. Sex).[38] Ultimately, *Love Me Tonight* celebrates the former and its main characters seem to reject the latter.

Mamoulian, prone to challenge the Pre-Code rules, found an ingenious way in *Love Me Tonight* to show an unmarried couple (Maurice and Jeanette) in bed together through a split screen double shot as the Princess and the tailor sing their passionate love duet "Love Me Tonight" via voice-over. Only Ontario objected to this suggestive frame in 1932, and Breen, who seemed to be concentrating on Myrna Loy's nightgown, didn't object to the vision of a young couple who weren't married sharing a bed on screen. This doesn't mean that we should infer he *approved* of Mamoulian's visual shenanigans, but no evidence survives that expressly reveals his displeasure about this particular breach of decorum.

This chapter has noted several memos in which Joy expressed his reservations about the lyrics to "A Woman Needs Something Like That." As early as his letter of March 8, 1932, he worried that the song may have gone "too far beyond the line between the risqué into the suggestive." After reading the Buff Script, Joy revisited his reservations (which he refers to as questions) about this song "from a Code and censorship point of view" to Schulberg on April 4 and 5. After viewing the completed film he wrote to Schulberg again on August 9 to express his worry that "some of the official censors may question some of the lines in the Doctor's song" and to Fitzgerald on August 11 to consider changing a few objectionable lyrics. In the end, Paramount took its chances and lost in a few places where state censorship boards requested the removal of the song's final stanza (beginning with "A doorbell needs tinkling/ A flower needs sprinkling,/And a woman needs something like that"). These were same lines of the song Joy singled out as objectionable. On the positive side of the ledger, although the boards in Ohio and British Columbia objected to parts of the Doctor's song, only the Australian board requested the removal of the "whole of girl's examination and conversation," that is, the complete removal of a song that includes considerable amounts of informative dialogue and is crucial to the development of the plot.[39]

Seventeen years later on October 20 Breen took Australia's cue and demanded the total elimination of "A Woman Needs Something Like That," "the Doctor's song." Unquestionably, Breen's command to excise this song is the most Draconian of his three conditions that had to be met "in order to make this picture acceptable for limited reissue in restricted type[s] of theatre[s]." But for reasons that are unclear the song was not removed, a cause for celebration. Somewhat surprisingly, despite Breen's hostility to the film and PCA's directive, viewers in 1949 were able to see most of "A Woman Needs Something Like That." Viewers today who have access to the 2003 DVD or internet screenings can enjoy the same privilege.

The scene did not come away totally unscathed, however. As originally filmed, "A Woman Needs Something Like That" begins with the Duke introducing the Doctor to Jeanette before leaving the Doctor and his patient alone. In rhymed speech Jeanette explains to the Doctor the imperative that she be examined only by a man of noble birth. Neither the screenplay nor the film resolves this issue, although in both the Doctor refers to Jeanette as "Your Highness." This address disregards requests made by Joy on March 29 in response to his reading of the Buff Script and Trotti on April 20 in response to his reading of the White Script. Instead, in the film rereleased in 1949 the scene cuts abruptly away from Jeanette's fainting spell to her bedroom where a Doctor asks Jeanette to remove her dress and assures her that "as long as professional ethics apply,/I'll see you with only a doctor's eye!" Jeanette removes her dress and "the doctor's eye is satisfied."

The rest of the scene, mostly spoken in rhythmic and rhymed speech, is retained unexpurgated and unaltered until the final stanza. During the course of the song viewers learn that Jeanette has been experiencing fainting spells (even before Maurice serenaded her with "Mimi" on a country road) and that she feels depressed when she's "alone in bed at night." As the Doctor continues his interrogation, viewers learn that the Princess, now twenty-two, was married at the age of sixteen to a man of seventy-two who died three years later. The innuendo is clear that the marriage had not been consummated and that the reason she is "wasting away" is because she has been unfulfilled sexually, both during her marriage and her three years of widowhood.[40] At the end of the song, the Doctor, without directly stating his diagnosis, reveals the cure to the Duke: the "Princess ought to be married" and "to a man of her own age."

The retention of most of "A Woman Needs Something Like That" was in direct defiance of the conditions set by Breen and the Production Code. We may never know for sure how and why most of this song managed to slip by Breen's watchful eye. But to place the dance between the studios and the Production Code it should be noted that the former frequently took their chances and often got away with material that had been forbidden by the latter during the script negotiations and subsequently left mercifully unchecked when the film was screened and certificated prior to release.[41]

In comparing Joseph I. Breen's approach to films with that of his predecessor Colonel Joy, Vieira criticizes the failure of Joy's successor to acknowledge that some films containing sexual or other controversial elements "were works of art." Vieira continues: "Breen was as skilled a story editor as Jason Joy, but he did not share Joy's respect for cinematic accomplishment. Breen only had one goal—to impose his moral values on the film industry."[42] On some occasions, for example the intense negotiations over the retention of the rape scene in the film version of *A Streetcar Named Desire* (Warner Bros., 1951), Breen at least recognized the prestige of playwright Tennessee Williams and director Elia Kazan, and after they voiced a well-reasoned argument, found a way (if not to Williams's full satisfaction) to allow the rape scene by creating some ambiguity concerning its aftermath.[43]

Sexual Content in *Love Me Tonight* and the Unwritten Twenty-first-Century Production Code

Viewers of *Love Me Tonight* do not see a rape. The film contains no nudity, no sexual scenes of any kind, and just the bare minimum of kissing. On the

Figure 4.2 Maurice Chevalier measuring Jeanette MacDonald for her new riding habit.

other hand, Maurice does nonchalantly touch Jeanette's bust when measuring her for a riding habit as shown in Figure 4.2.[44]

Through the magic of split-screen photography, the two lovers also clearly appear to inhabit the same bed and the same film frame as their off-stage voices sing "Love Me Tonight." Fortunately, the only objection to this provocation came from Ontario, the major spoilsport among the censorship boards. When he first received the lyrics to "Love Me Tonight" in March, Joy found the lyric "must we sleep tonight alone" "questionable," which prompted Lasky to propose an alternative, but as noted, the song's verse that contains this lyric and remains in the published lyric, in the end was not filmed. But of far greater significance than this lyric, viewers then and now can clearly observe that Jeanette and Maurice are not sleeping alone (see Figure 4.3).

By 1932, viewers had already seen Jeanette MacDonald's underclothes in earlier films, but they were neither transparent, low cut, nor otherwise particularly revealing. Before allowing the film's limited rerelease in 1949, Breen prohibited audiences from catching even a glimpse of Myrna Loy's legs underneath her translucent nightgown. What remains was sophisticated innuendo and one of the sexiest films imaginable without showing any sex.

Figure 4.3 Maurice and Jeanette singing "Love Me Tonight" in a two shot in separate beds.

No doubt Joy and Breen noticed potentially suggestive lyrics, lines of dialogue, and visual images that they allowed without comment or challenge. For example, theater historian Miles Kreuger in his informative and insightful audio commentary included as a special feature on the 2003 DVD, adds a previously unremarked potential instance of possible sexual visual innuendo. What Kreuger noticed and called attention to was the viewer's first shot of Maurice with his "head penetrating the neck of his skin-tight sweater."[45] Was Mamoulian deliberately being sexually suggestive or is Kreuger reading too much into an innocuous image? Since neither Joy nor Breen weighed in on this scene, viewers can decide for themselves.

In any event, a few moments later in "The Song of Paree," the narrative raises the possibility that two of the women the tailor meets on the way to his shop apparently may have had opportunities to discover whether Kreuger was on the right track. After Maurice asks one girl on the street "How about Friday?" and a second girl interjects with annoyance "Friday is my day!" viewers can form their own conclusions about what happens on Friday nights in Maurice's apartment.[46]

Maurice first encounters Jeanette after her carriage has gone into a ditch on a country road. Immediately he is smitten. When he goes to help her, he doesn't say "let me help you," he says, "Mademoiselle, put your arms around me." When Jeanette asks Maurice, not without some irritation, whether he thinks she puts her arms around strangers, he responds immediately by telling her his name, thus making him no longer a stranger. He then offers to massage her ankle. When Jeanette rejects this goodwill gesture, Maurice asks for a moment of her time so that he can sing a song to the woman he insists on calling Mimi.

The concluding lyric of "Mimi" is both bold and revealing: "You know I'd like to have a little son of a Mimi, by and by." This lyric, which only the prudish censors at Ontario asked to remove, comes across as presumptuous (by the reaction shot of Jeanette's face, she clearly thinks so). But what made the lyric especially provocative was that it was accompanied by a seemingly suggestive leer from Chevalier as he looks at Jeanette's belly. To put a positive spin on this leer, it reveals that Maurice wants something more than casual sex, but a leer is still a leer. Still, by the time he sang "Mimi," Maurice has informed viewers in "Isn't It Romantic?" that he thinks "kiddies are romantic," although at the same time he frames the idea of having a troupe of children as an altruistic act to "help the population" and "a duty that we owe to France."

In his indispensable discussion of the three musical film genres (the fairy tale musical the show musical, and the folk musical), Rick Altman demonstrates the way *Love Me Tonight* can be classified as a fairy tale musical.[47] In Altman's analysis, the plot of a fairy tale musical "must so organize things that initial concern for birth or fortune become secondary to a skill which the postulant character possesses."[48] After citing Fred Astaire's dancing and Nelson Eddy's singing as iconic skills that carried them through a series of fairy tale musicals in the years immediately following *Love Me Tonight,* Altman asserts that Chevalier's skill "is that well known Gallic charm (read s-e-x)" and supports this assertion by quoting the description on the completed tapestry stitched by Jeanette's three eccentric Aunts throughout the movie and revealed in the final frame accompanied by the words, "Once upon a time there was a Princess and a Prince Charming, who was not a Prince, but who was charming . . . and they lived happily ever after."[49]

Indeed, the charming (but not princely) Maurice charms nearly all the residents of the chateau, from the noble Duke to the lowly chambermaid. As the Duke explains, Maurice is the first of Gilbert's friends he doesn't want "to hit with a battle axe," and before she learned that Maurice was a tailor, not a Baron, the chambermaid "used to *flirt* until it *hurt,* while he stood there in his *undershirt.*" Within the first minute of their meeting Valentine wants to show Maurice the Virgin's Spring. Yet Jeanette, the only person at the chateau (other than Maurice's putative romantic rival the Count) who can resist the tailor's contagious and ubiquitous charm, is the only woman Maurice desires. The subtext of "A Woman Needs Something Like That" is that sex will be the foundation of Maurice's appeal and that Jeanette is a woman in need. The something she needs is not unlike what Scarlett O'Hara's lover, then husband, Rhett Butler thinks Scarlett needs in *Gone with the Wind* (1939): she "should be kissed and often, and by someone who knows how."[50]

We are persuaded that Jeanette is the only woman for Maurice because of the way he resists the man-hungry and sexually desirable Valentine, who has clearly made herself available to him. The fact that it takes Jeanette some time to come around to Maurice is also part of the fairy tale trope. As Altman explains, "Whatever the source of the commoner's charm—fancy foot-work, a way with a tune, or simply sexual prowess—the refusal of the pro-spective partner to fall immediately prey remains a necessary plot device."[51] Eventually, by the time we reach the title love song, it's clear that Maurice's love is reciprocated. All that remains is for Jeanette to overcome the class dis-parity that separates the two lovers. Not to worry. In a fairy tale, musical love will conquer all, even the moving train that the Princess heroically stops to reunite with her tailor at story's end.

Maurice's absurd rival for Jeanette, the Count, is never a serious threat. We first meet him standing on top of a ladder in Jeanette's bedroom window immediately after she has sung the conclusion of "Isn't It Romantic?" having fallen in love with her future Prince Charming at "first sound." Before he falls on his flute (a suggestive line reliably rejected in Ontario), the Count's re-sponse when Jeanette tells him she is going to bed is that he "just came up to join you [her]" and that he brought his flute with him "hoping to entertain."

In a conversation a little later, the Count misunderstands Gilbert's non se-quitur about his elder brother, a nipomaniac, a play on the word kleptoma-niac. In the context of their conversation a nipomaniac (a word not available in a game of Scrabble) is someone who pinches (i.e., steals) things. This is the cue for the Count to recall a friend who "used to pinch business girls in elevators" and consequently was sent to a cooler climate. Although the Count's recollection of his friend was banished only in Ontario in 1932, a casual mention of someone committing serial sexual assaults in public places like this would certainly be impermissible in today's social climate.

And then there's Valentine, whom viewers first meet when Jeanette returns to the chateau and falls into a faint after meeting Maurice in a countryside ditch. When viewers first see Valentine, she is in the middle of an entryway, having fallen asleep out of sheer boredom. In his efforts to revive Jeanette,

Gilbert wakes up his cousin to ask whether she can "go for a doctor." As recorded in chapter 1, Valentine responds with alacrity and tells Gilbert to "bring him right in."

When she first meets Maurice a little later, Valentine doesn't waste time, immediately asking him whether he is married. Upon learning that he is not, she says without hesitation that she'll be right down to take him to the Virgin's Spring. Valentine may not be a nipomaniac, but it was unusual for a woman outside of a Hollywood film to be so open about her romantic interests even during the Pre-Code era. Valentine's uninhibited sexual nature is most clearly evident in an exchange with her rival Jeanette shortly before the hunt. What prompts Valentine's first question is that Jeanette has given the uppity tailor masquerading as a Baron the uncontrollably volatile horse named Solitude to ride in the hunt, in order to give him a comeuppance.

VALENTINE: What is the point in giving the Baron a horse like that?
JEANETTE: I want to test the Baron.
VALENTINE: I could think of several better ways to do that. Let me try.
JEANETTE: Don't bother. Tell me, do you ever think of anything but men, dear?
  Valentine: Oh, yes.
JEANETTE: Of what?
VALENTINE: Schoolboys.

Altman notes that "until 1934 Hollywood enjoyed a nearly European freedom in its choice of subject, treatments, dialogue, etc."[52] Valentine's response to Jeanette is a telling example of this Pre-Code sensibility. Curiously, not even Ontario objected to the implications that Valentine had "better ways" to test Maurice, who at this point in the story has convinced everyone except the Count that he is a Baron. Perhaps more surprisingly, Breen himself seems not to have objected to Valentine's remark about schoolboys. But as Cole Porter begins his song "Anything Goes," "Times have changed." In the current millennium Valentine's flippancy might arguably brand her as a sexual predator and therefore less palatable to evolving moral values.

One review of the original 1932 release of *Love Me Tonight* described it as "an outstanding motion picture achievement," a film that "will drive your cares away as swiftly and surely as a bubbling bottle of champagne, and with no unpleasant after effects."[53] Writing for a putatively provincial newspaper in upstate New York near the Canadian border, the reviewer responded to the sexual innuendo in an imaginary French dialect, "This *Love Me Tonight*—eet ees veree naughtee! But it is also very subtle, thus avoiding the vaguest hint of vulgarity."

Table 4.1 Censorship and *Love Me Tonight*: Original Release (August 18, 1932) and Rerelease (1949)

STUDIO RELATIONS COMMITTEE (SRC) RECOMMENDATIONS AND PARAMOUNT'S RESPONSE

Lyrics:

"The Song of Paree"

- SRC Recommendation (1/28): To remove the expression "thank God."
  Paramount Action: Expression "thank God" removed.

"Isn't It Romantic?"

- SRC Recommendation (4/19): To omit "for France" in the lyric, "We would rather sing than fight for France."
  Paramount Action: Lyric retained.

"A Woman Needs Something Like That"

- SRC Recommendation (3/7): To consider the possibility whether the studio has gone "beyond the line between the risqué into the suggestive."
  Paramount Action: Lyric retained.

- SRC Recommendation (4/20): "The Doctor's song is still dubious, although as we said before perhaps it will be far less so when it is recorded." No specific recommendation.
  Paramount Action: Lyric retained.

"The Poor Apache"

- SRC Recommendation (8/9): Warning about possible elimination of "nuts to you" by state censors.
  Paramount Action: Lyric retained.

"Love Me Tonight"

- SRC Recommendation (3/9): To consider the "questionable" lyric, "Must we sleep tonight all alone?"
  Paramount Action: Lyric retained.

Dialogue: Buff Script (March 26)

- SRC Recommendation (3/28): To remove innuendo in the dialogue and lyrics to *"A Woman Needs Something Like That."*
  Paramount Action: None.

- SRC Recommendation (3/28): To remove references to Bastille Day.
  SRC Recommendation (3/29): Recommendation withdrawn.
  Paramount Action: References to Bastille Day removed.

- SRC Recommendation (3/29): To refrain from addressing Princess Jeanette as "Your Highness"
  Paramount Action: Expression "Your Highness" removed but not until after the submission of the White Script.

- SRC Recommendation (3/39): To omit scene of the Princess striking a servant with her riding whip.
  Paramount Action: Scene removed.

Table 4.1 Continued

Dialogue: White Script (April 19)

- SRC Recommendation (4/5): Question remains about "A Woman Needs Something Like That" but no specific request to alter either the sung or spoken portions of the song. Paramount Action: None.

- SRC Recommendation (4/20): Request to remove the scene in which "Gilbert— wearing only shorts, undershirt and shoes—is caught in a room with a woman who is reclining on a bed."
Paramount Action: Scene removed.

- SRC Recommendation (4/20): "There is still the question of addressing the Princess as 'Your Highness.'"
Paramount Action: Delayed removal of the address "Your Highness."

State Censorship Boards (August 24–December 2, 1932)
(Film footage with the words in bold also deleted in 1949 rerelease.)

"APPROVED WITHOUT ELIMINATIONS"

The original 1932 release of *Love Me Tonight* was "Approved without eliminations" by the following US state and Canadian province censorship boards:

Kansas (September 6) New York (September 22) Chicago (October 18)[a] Quebec (November 3)

What follows is a list of lyrics, dialogues, and film frames removed from versions of *Love Me Tonight* shown in various states in the US and Canadian provinces.

ELIMINATED LYRICS (1932)

"The Song of Paree"

> Girl: I need a beau.
> Maurice: Where's your husband?
> Girl: He needs the dough.
> Ontario, Canada (October 12)

"Isn't It Romantic?"

> Maurice: "When I take a shower/She can scrub my back" to "We'll help the population:/It's a duty that we owe to France."
> Ontario, Canada (October 12)

"Mimi"

> "You know I'd like to/Have a little/Son of a Mimi,/By and by."
> Ontario, Canada (October 12)

"A Woman Needs Something Like That"[b]

> Doctor: "With eyes and red lips/And a figure like that!/You're not wasted away—/You're just wasted" to **"A drum must be beaten,/And a woman needs something like that! Madame!"**[c]
> Ohio (September 16)

> Doctor: "With eyes and red lips, and a figure like that, you're not wasted away. You're just wasted!"
> Ohio (reinserted October 3)

> **Doctor: "A doorbell needs tinkling"** to "To keep in condition/And a woman needs something like that!"
> British Columbia (October 3)

> "Whole of girl's examination and conversation—etc. with doctor"
> Australia (December 2)

(continued)

Table 4.1 Continued

"Mimi" (reprise)

> "You know I'd like to/Have a little/Son of a Mimi/by and by."
>> Ontario, Canada (October 12)

> "Eliminate ripping noise after Count sings song 'Mimi' while exercising with dumbbells."
>> Pennsylvania (September 28)

> "Eliminate sound of rip."
>> British Columbia (October 3)

"The Poor Apache"

> "The spot that no one dare touch,/the spot that only chairs touch,/Is frequently touching the ground!"[d]
>> British Columbia (October 3)

> Eliminate "only for Sunday showing": "I didn't know my mother,/Who didn't know my father,/My parents were not well acquainted!"
>> Massachusetts (August 24)

> "To master a wench/with a hammer and wrench"
>> Ontario, Canada (October 12)

"The Son-of-a-Gun Is Nothing but a Tailor"
> Chambermaid: I used to flirt/Until it hurt,/While he stood there/In his undershirt!
>> British Columbia (October 3)

ELIMINATED DIALOGUE (1932)

Gilbert: He may come along any minute.
Maurice: Who?
> British Columbia (October 3)

Gilbert: The girl's husband, he came home unexpectedly.[e]
Maurice: What girl?
Gilbert: Well, she's—uh-uh—well, I don't remember. The husband started running after me, and I ran and somehow, I found myself in a race.
> Pennsylvania (September 28) British Columbia (October 3) Ontario, Canada (October 12) British (October 26)

Count: Oh, I'll never be able to use it again.
Jeanette: Oh, Count, did you break your leg?
Count: No, I fell flat on my flute.[f]
> Ontario, Canada (October 12)

Maurice: You are not the man who chased the Vicomte in his B.V.D.'s?
Man: Certainly not.
> Ontario, Canada (October 12)

Count: "He used to pinch business girls in elevators. They had to send him to a cooler climate."
> Ontario, Canada (October 12)

Doctor: From "But the Princess ought to be ought to be married" to "Well, well, this is a problem."
> Ontario, Canada (October 12)

Table 4.1 Continued

Count: From: "I'll ask her to consider me as a prescription" to "I didn't know there was
1 one in the neighborhood."
    Ontario, Canada (October 12)[g]

I didn't know there was one in this [the] neighborhood.
    Australia (December 2)

**Valentine: Oh! Too bad you didn't get here sooner. I've had everybody out showing
them the Virgin's Spring.**
Maurice: The what, Mademoiselle?
Valentine: The Virgin's Spring. I tell you what. I'll show it to you privately.
Maurice: Is it a new dance?
Valentine: No, no – it's a spring of water.[h]
Maurice: Yes?
Valentine: Tonight, if there's a moon.[i]
Maurice: Oh!
Valentine: Are you alone?
Maurice: Alone?
Valentine: I mean in life. You're not married?
Maurice: Ah, no.
Valentine: I'll be right down.
    Ohio (September 16)

Count: "... including the high class illegitimates" [the better class illegitimates]
    Australia (December 2)

Count: At her age? Remarkable!
Gilbert: Huh! The old girl must have something!
    Pennsylvania (September 28)[j]

ELIMINATED FILM FRAMES (1932)

"Maurice taking Jeanette's bust measure"
    Alberta (October 3)

"View showing head of man and woman on pillows side by side" ("Love Me
Tonight" voice over)
"Shorten view of Maurice and Jeannette [sic] kissing"
    Ontario, Canada (October 12)

---

[a] Before crossing out the requests, the Chicago censor board had proposed the elimination of the dialogue passages when Gilbert is discovered in bed with another man's wife and the conversation about the Virgin's Spring as well as the lyric in "The Poor Apache" that contains the line that Maurice's "parents were not well acquainted."

[b] The request to eliminate the material from "And now, my dear, remove your dress" to the end of the song was crossed out in the Ontario, Canada directive of October 12.

[c] The 1949 reissue deleted all lines from "You're just wasted" until the end of the song.

[d] The censors in Ontario, Canada (October 12), requested a long elimination from "While other men are dancing" to "My parents were not acquainted!" for a total of nineteen consecutive lines in the lyrics.

[e] The dialogue that included the material about "The girl's husband" was also removed from the film's trailer in British Columbia (October 3).

(continued)

Table 4.1 Continued

---

[f] This line was also removed when the Count repeated it at the Ball later in the film.

[g] The last portion of the deleted passage from "Are you ready?" to "I didn't know there was one in the neighborhood" and the material from "Too bad you didn't get here sooner" to "Tonight, if there's a moon" were removed in the 1949 rerelease. The dialogue from "Are you alone?" to "I'll be right down" was preserved. See the section on "Deletions in 1949" in this table.

[h] "Is it a new dance? And "No, no—it's a spring of water" is not expressly deleted by the Ohio censors.

[i] The censorship board in British Columbia (October 3) eliminated from "I've had everybody out showing" to "Tonight, if there's a moon" and the three references to the word "Virgin."

[j] The single line "The old girl must have something" was removed in the Australian print (December 2).

5

The Reception of *Love Me Tonight* from Its Time to Ours

"There is more creative pleasure in 1932's 89-minute *Love Me Tonight*
than in all the endless hours of late 1960s musicals combined."

Matthew Kennedy, *Roadshow! The Fall of
Film Musicals in the 1960s.*

1932

Love Me Tonight arrived several years after the explosion of film musicals
that marked the early years of the sound film, with more than sixty musicals
released in 1929 and more than eighty in 1930. When the taste for film
musicals plunged along with the stock market, the fall was both swift and
staggering. Only eleven film musicals opened in 1931, and of these only two
made money.[1] In 1932, when Paramount suffered a deficit of $16 million, the
grand total of musicals was again eleven, seven of which were produced by
Paramount, including two musicals that questionably deserved this designation.[2] Included in this number were two Chevalier–MacDonald pairings,
One Hour with You and *Love Me Tonight*. The following year things started
looking up when *42nd Street* came along to launch a popular and financially
successful series of Busby Berkeley dance musicals. Also in 1933, the inaugu-
ration of the historic Astaire and Rogers partnership with *Flying Down to Rio*
would greatly contribute to the popularization of dance in film musicals for
the rest of the decade.

Most of the nearly forty contemporary reviews of *Love Me Tonight* col-
lected in typescript in the "Press Reviews 1932–33" folder of the Mamoulian
Collection are laudatory. This chapter will offer only a few highlights.
Mordaunt Hall of the *New York Times* may have started the bandwagon by
comparing Mamoulian (not especially favorably) to the French director
René Clair and the German-born Lubitsch: "Although he may not reveal

Love Me Tonight. Geoffrey Block, Oxford University Press. © Oxford University Press 2024.
DOI: 10.1093/9780197566220.003.0005

Ernst Lubitsch's satire and keen wit or Rene [René] Clair's clever irony, he, in a somewhat precise and often theatric fashion gives to his scenes a charming poetic suggestion."[3] Perhaps surprisingly, only one other review in the Press Review folder mentions Clair: "The opening sequences representing the awakening of Paris are the apotheosis of cinema rhythm, and go beyond anything of the kind that Rene [René] Clair or Walt Disney or Lubitsch has given us."[4]

One, but only one, of the Press Reviews noted the origins of *Love Me Tonight*'s opening in the play *Porgy*. The author of this thoughtful review, William F. McDermott, also demonstrated a solid grasp of Mamoulian's objectives: "Roughly speaking, the Mamoulian method is to substitute stylization and synochronization [*sic*] of sound and movement for literal realism."[5] The title of a review in the *Seattle Times* just about says it all: "Chevalier Film One of Screen's Real Triumphs: 'Love Me Tonight' Praised for Scintillating Wit, Fine Directions, Brilliant Cast and Lavish Settings."[6] The title and the text of this review covers a high number of the film's virtues as its author enthusiastically proclaims: "as near perfect a bit of screen entertainment as I have seen in all my experiences as a moviegoer is Maurice Chevalier's new cinema 'Love Me Tonight.'" The title and text also reinforce the prevailing idea that the reviewer was reviewing a *Chevalier* film, not a Mamoulian film.

Given his popularity at the time, it is not surprising that Chevalier's name appears in thirteen review titles while Mamoulian's appears in only four (plus a fifth in which readers must figure out for themselves that Mamoulian was the "Satirist from Armenia"). Upon the French release of the film in October, French reviewers, like their American counterparts, also tended to describe the film as a "Chevalier picture." Joseph Horowitz notes an exception that appeared in the *La Cinématographie Française*: "Mamoulian has fashioned . . . a masterpiece of grace, charm, spirit, and also novel technique. By structuring his film in a continuous balletic mode, by his use of sound as a means of expression, by the ongoing research into staging, Mamoulian has truly created a new style of musical cinema."[7]

Some of the early American reviews as well did express their admiration for Mamoulian's accomplishment, even if his name does not appear in the title or directly in the text:

Here is a picture which, in its own way, touches perfection. From its beginning, when before your eyes and to your ears, the city of Paris wakes up, its characteristic sounds woven into music, to its end which is like that of all fairy tales, it is a thing of romance, humor, beauty with the lilt of melody through it.

> Genevieve Harris, "Chevalier Picture Is Rare Entertainment,"
> *Chicago Post,* n.d.

"Love Me Tonight" is a delightful concoction of comedy, sentiment, music and fantasy, and Rouben Mamoulian has succeeded in combining these four ingredients into one of the outstanding productions of its type in recent years.

> "'Love Me Tonight' Full of Comedy, Sentiment, Music and Fantasy,"
> *Richmond News-Leader,* September 10, 1932.

Again, "Love Me Tonight" had an extraordinary freshness, a lyrical quality which took you out of yourself, which fulfilled the first requirement of a work of art, namely to give pleasure, and compel your submission to the illusion. And so, for originality, imagination, beauty, freshness, and wit, I single out the work of Mamoulian.

> "Ernest Betts Picks 'Love Me Tonight,'" *The Era* (London),
> December 30, 1932.

Despite such consistently positive reviews, *Love Me Tonight,* which cost $1.1 million, like most Depression musicals of 1931 and 1932, lost an undisclosed amount of money on its investment. The loss was not so much due to its lack of popularity but to the many delays that required the studio to reimburse Chevalier for engagements previously made, engagements that his contractual obligations to Paramount did not allow him to fulfill.[8]

After 1932 to the Present

Rick Altman's claim to the contrary, after its rerelease in 1949, Mamoulian's film virtually vanished from public view until its simultaneous distribution on VHS and DVD in 2003.[9] In this respect the fate of *Love Me Tonight* was not unlike the neglect endured by Lubitsch's four continental fairy tale musicals from 1929 to 1932, none of which became commercially available on DVD until 2008. The *public* neglect of *Love Me Tonight* did not, however, mean that no one noticed the film. Quite the contrary. As early as the article "Music in the Movies" that appeared in *Harper's Bazaar* in 1946, before the film's rerelease in 1949, Kurt Weill wrote that "Rouben Mamoulian, with the help of Rodgers and Hart, created in *Love Me Tonight* a really intelligent, uncompromising musical picture which has become a kind of classic of its genre."[10] This final chapter will privilege Chevalier, MacDonald, and Mamoulian, but Weill's singling out of Rodgers and Hart offers a welcome reminder that the score has been consistently (and rightfully) regarded as one of the great film scores of the 1930s and beyond.

A significant factor in the history of *Love Me Tonight's* reception is the fact that it inspired an impressive array of influential makers of film musicals in the 1940s and 1950s. One of these was Vincente Minnelli, who, looking back on his first years at Paramount in the early 1940s, recalled that he "would often look at Mamoulian's *Love Me Tonight*, as it was such a perfect example of how to make a musical."[11] The panoramic view of Paris that opens *An American in Paris* (1951) is perhaps the best evidence that Minnelli had not forgotten the opening of *Love Me Tonight*.[12] According to film historian John Kobal, Arthur Freed and Charles Walters, like Minnelli, "agreed that *Love Me Tonight* had the greatest influence on their own work."[13] Stanley Donen, co-director of *On the Town* and *Singin' in the Rain,* recalled telling Mamoulian that he frequently viewed *Love Me Tonight* before embarking on a new film.[14] Presumably Minnelli, Walters, and Donen had special access to private prints in order to screen films like *Love Me Tonight* that were not generally available for public viewing.

In summarizing Mamoulian's career, Hugh Fordin writes that the director "is part of the lives of millions of people who have never heard of him."[15] The comparison may seem far-fetched, but directors like Minnelli, Walters, and Donen and producers like Freed viewed Mamoulian with the same reverence that Franz Joseph Haydn, Wolfgang Amadeus Mozart, and Ludwig van Beethoven viewed J. S. Bach. In a situation analogous to Mamoulian, widely known as a stage director who didn't enjoy a high profile as a film director in his lifetime but *was* known to many great film directors who followed, Bach was known in his lifetime almost exclusively as an organist while his compositions moved underground and virtually disappeared for more than a half century after his death in 1750.

Yet somehow the composers who led music into the future *did* discover Bach and learned a great deal from him. Consequently, they were able to compensate for the neglect. Haydn discovered Bach late in his compositional career but in time to influence the two great oratorios, *The Creation* (1798) and *The Seasons* (1801), and his six late masses. Not long after settling in Vienna in 1782, Mozart reported in a letter to his father that every Sunday at noon he attended concerts sponsored by Baron Gottfried van Swieten at the Imperial Library "where nothing is played but Handel and Bach."[16] Bach was little known in Beethoven's hometown of Bonn until Beethoven's teacher Christian Gottlob Neefe, trained in Bach's hometown of Leipzig, brought Bach to Bonn, shared the master's compositions with his new student, then only twelve, and reported on this fact in an article published in 1783: "I need say no more than that the chief piece he [Beethoven] plays is The Well-Tempered Clavier of Sebastian Bach."[17] Although not a household name to the general public, Mamoulian was the film director's Bach, especially when it came to his 1930s films like *Love Me Tonight*.

For those who recognized his name, Mamoulian was remembered mainly as the stage director of *Porgy and Bess*, *Oklahoma!*, and *Carousel*. The general public had largely forgotten Mamoulian's films in the 1940s and early 1950s before his comeback with *Silk Stockings* in 1957. Nevertheless, his achievements in his sixteen films, especially *Love Me Tonight,* remained an influence as well as an inspiration to his peers, much as Bach's music, largely unknown, influenced and inspired the most significant composers who followed in the years immediately after Bach's death.[18] Film directors who followed in Mamoulian's footsteps knew the director's work and what it meant to them and the future of film, just as Haydn, Mozart, and Beethoven knew what Bach meant to music.

Mark N. Grant is not alone in his conclusion, previously quoted in chapter 2, that *Love Me Tonight* is "arguably the first completely integrated musical comedy on stage or screen."[19] Nevertheless, despite its visual imagination, technical innovation, captivating story, widely revered musical score, and stellar cast, *Love Me Tonight* has also provoked some dissent, perhaps most notably from the influential movie critic Andrew Sarris, who famously wrote that "Mamoulian's tragedy" was "that of an innovator who runs out of innovations."[20] Sarris, who regarded Mamoulian as a director who was hopelessly dated (by 1968), also dismissed *Love Me Tonight* as "imitation Lubitsch with too many camera angles."[21]

Decades later, David Thomson, while giving *Love Me Tonight* credit for an "hour of originality," found the film "a little too unrelenting to be appealing" and concluded that the individually "fetching" details "do not add up and that the invention is glitteringly ostentatious."[22] Others have criticized the film for its lack of dancing, which is largely absent from both Lubitsch and

Mamoulian musicals of the 1930s but which would shortly return to the screen in the films of Berkeley and Astaire and Rogers. Early film historian Richard Barrios accepts this charge but defends the absence of dance: "If the performers don't dance, Mamoulian sees to it that the photography and editing and soundtrack all do."[23]

Despite these reservations, the critical verdict on *Love Me Tonight* has remained consistently high. The Preface quoted superlatives from film critics Leonard Maltin and Barrios, but it may be worth repeating in this final chapter that the former proclaims *Love Me Tonight* as "one of the best musicals ever made" and the latter extols the film as "one of the finest ever written for motion pictures."[24] In their survey of Chevalier films Gene Ringgold and Dewitt Bodeen write that "no discerning film student or scholar disputes the word-of-mouth acclaim which now justly decrees it the all-time best screen musical" and asks wistfully, "if there is a better musical of the Thirties, one wonders what it can be."[25] It was also noted in the Preface that a much later survey published in 2019 by Jeanine Basinger reinforces the prevailing position of past film directors, historians, and critics when she concludes that *Love Me Tonight* has "never really been surpassed for its organic integration of music, plot, and character."[26]

Several writers compare Mamoulian's accomplishment favorably with that of the generally more highly acclaimed Lubitsch, starting with Mamoulian scholar Tom Milne, who assesses *Love Me Tonight* as "one of the most enchanting musicals ever made, the Lubitsch film that Lubitsch was always trying to pull off but never quite did."[27] In his comprehensive film survey of 1930s film musicals, John Baxter also favored *Love Me Tonight* over Lubitsch musicals: "Gay, charming, witty, it is everything that the Lubitsch musicals should have been but never were."[28] Edwin M. Bradley described *Love Me Tonight* as "a movie that out-Lubitsched Lubitsch" and "one of the most cohesive, adventurous musicals of all time."[29] Milne may have a bias that tilts toward his principal subject, but Baxter and Bradley took into account virtually every sound film that appeared before 1933.

None of these comparisons with Lubitsch factor the outstanding and memorable Rodgers and Hart score from *Love Me Tonight* that more than out-Lubitsched the serviceable and effective but ultimately less memorable musical scores Lubitsch commissioned for his films.[30] Not until his final musical, *The Merry Widow* (1934) with music already composed by Franz Lehár, was Lubitsch's imagination supported by a timeless musical score.

Also siding with Mamoulian in the Lubitsch–Mamoulian debate is Barrios, who, in his survey of sound films argues that in comparison with Lubitsch, in which the earlier Chevalier–MacDonald pairings tend to treat infidelity and even romance lightly, in *Love Me Tonight* their roles "develop deeper characterizations than in their previous films, chiefly because the slyness and sexual skirmishes are coupled for the first time with genuine romance."[31] Finally, in his magisterial survey of romantic film comedies between 1929 and 1948, both musical and nonmusical, from Lubitsch to Preston Sturges, James Harvey pays the following tribute to Mamoulian: "A strange footnote to this period in the Lubitsch career is the fact that the Chevalier-MacDonald movie which probably most people think of as the pinnacle of the Lubitsch style, is not by Lubitsch but by Rouben Mamoulian, that most eclectic of gifted thirties directors: *Love Me Tonight* (1932)."[32]

Some of the praise for *Love Me Tonight* appears in unlikely places. The epigraph by Matthew Kennedy that introduces this chapter offers a prime example: "There is more creative pleasure in 1932's 89-minute *Love Me Tonight* than in all the endless hours of late 1960s musicals combined."[33] This is the kind of statement one might expect to find in the previously mentioned books on film musicals of the late 1920s and 1930s by Bradley, Baxter, Barrios, or Harvey, but the surprising source of the quotation is a book on *1960s* musicals. After extolling the virtues of such musical film classics as *The Wizard of Oz, An American in Paris*, and collectively the films of Gene Kelly, Fred Astaire, and Judy Garland Kennedy, the author of *Roadshow! The Fall of the Film Musicals in the 1960s,* confesses that he has "reconciled my childhood memories of the late 1960s musicals with the adult realization that most of them aren't very good."[34] What follows is an excellent survey of its subject, but as Kennedy admits at the outset, the author's lot is not always a happy one.

A final unlikely source of critical praise for *Love Me Tonight* comes from Stephen Sondheim in an interview with Jesse Green from 2007 that took place in connection with the then recently released film adaptation of *Sweeney Todd*. During the course of the interview Sondheim recalled that "the only kind of movie I didn't like as a kid were musicals" and that he found the four film adaptations of his stage musicals prior to *Sweeney Todd* (*West Side Story, Gypsy, A Funny Thing Happened on the Way to the Forum*, and *A Little Night Music*) all unsatisfactory.[35] In a public interview in Portland, Oregon, with Frank Rich a few months later, Sondheim shared his view that the recent film adaptation of *Sweeney Todd* was not only the first decent adaptation of a Sondheim show but "the most satisfactory film made of any stage musical."[36] Given Sondheim's displeasure with film musicals as a genre "as a kid" and the adaptations of his own stage musicals prior to *Sweeney Todd* it is all the more remarkable that, aside from "a couple" of unnamed MGM musicals, Sondheim was able to mention only three movie musicals he enjoys.[37] Significantly, none of the musicals on his short list are adaptations of stage musicals. Sondheim doesn't say if he is naming these films in order of preference, but the first film musical he mentions is *Love Me Tonight*.[38]

The triple-threat critic John Simon (film, theater, and music) made the following pronouncement on what makes a film great: "The surest way of testing a movie's greatness is seeing it a second time. If it is just as good, it is a good film. If it gets better in the fineness and fullness of its detail, it is great."[39] Having by now seen *Love Me Tonight* more than two times, I attest that this film musical fully meets Simon's criteria. It is a film worthy of the almost universally high regard it has received. This captivating musical fairy tale richly deserves to be better and more widely known. It also holds a unique place in American film musical history as a pioneering innovative, influential, controversial, yet enduring work of art.

Plot Summary

"Once upon a time there was a Princess and a Prince Charming . . . Who was not a Prince. But who was charming. And they lived happily ever after . . . "

LOVE ME TONIGHT tells the story of how a lowly but ambitious Parisian tailor, Maurice (Maurice Chevalier), discovers romance and love with Princess Jeanette (Jeanette MacDonald) at her country chateau. The story begins with the sounds and noises of Paris awakening **("Symphony of Noises")** and Maurice greeting fellow shopkeepers and other acquaintances on his way to open his shop for the day **("The Song of Paree")**. At his shop we meet Emile, a satisfied paying customer picking up his beautiful newly tailored wedding suit, and Gilbert, Vicomte de Varèze, who owes thousands of francs on a lavish wardrobe, borrowing on credit from an overly trusting Maurice. After Gilbert leaves, Emile's new suit inspires a song **("Isn't It Romantic?")** that will be passed around from Emile and Maurice to a taxi driver, a composer, a group of soldiers, a Gypsy [recte Roma] violinist, and finally to Jeanette, who has overheard Maurice's song from the balcony of her country chateau.

Soon we meet the chateau's other eccentric inhabitants: Jeanette's inept and inappropriate suitor, the Count de Savignac (Charles Butterworth), her uncle and lord of the chateau, the Duke d'Artelines (C. Aubrey Smith), her three elderly Aunts, and Gilbert's man-hungry cousin, Countess Valentine (Myrna Loy). Meanwhile in Paris, Maurice decides to travel by car to the chateau in order to personally collect the money due him for Gilbert's many unpaid suits. On a country road Maurice observes Jeanette in a horse-drawn carriage singing to her horse **("Lover")** before her carriage, horse, and Jeanette are thrown into a ditch. Maurice comes to the rescue, falls immediately in love with Jeanette, and serenades her using a name he has made up on the spot **("Mimi")**. Upon returning to the chateau, Jeanette falls into a faint and is seen by a doctor who concludes that only marriage with a man her own age will cure her condition **("A Woman Needs Something Like That")**.

Maurice arrives at the chateau to collect the money owed him but reluctantly agrees to protect Gilbert's future financial prospects by pretending to be a Baron. With impressive rapidity, Maurice wins nearly everyone over by his charm, from the Duke to the house servants. The only residents who resist Maurice's charms are Jeanette, who fights her initial attraction and growing feelings for the imposter, and the jealous Count, who spends hours in the library archives attempting to prove that the Baron Courtelin is a fraud and not of noble lineage.

The next morning the Duke, Gilbert, two of the Aunts, and even the Count wake up singing a reprise of "Mimi" before the deer hunt. Maurice has truly brought new life to the inhabitants of the stodgy and nearly comatose ancient castle.

During the instrumental hunt ballet (**"The Hunt"**) Maurice rescues the deer from the dogs and brings it inside a hunting lodge, a breach of etiquette that angers Jeanette. In the course of their argument Jeanette criticizes Maurice's lack of breeding and Maurice criticizes Jeanette's ungraceful riding habit and severe hairstyle. At the Ball that evening Maurice flouts ballroom protocol and arrives dressed as a Parisian Apache, a street tough, and proceeds to celebrate this renegade group in song (**"The Poor Apache"**). Despite her displeasure with Maurice's song and behavior, Jeanette realizes her feelings for her charming prince and overcomes her resistance. The lovers declare their love and kiss (**"Love Me Tonight"**).

Despite his good fortune, the next day Maurice can't control the tailor in him and manages to find fault with Jeanette's riding habit and to insult the seamstress who created it. The seamstress causes a disturbance that causes the Duke, Gilbert, the Count, and the Aunts to barge into Jeanette's room, where they find her in her underwear alone with Maurice. In an effort to extricate himself from this compromising position Maurice promises to make a new riding habit within two hours. The fact that Maurice succeeds in crafting a beautiful outfit makes Jeanette become suspicious, and she demands the truth about how he was able to accomplish this unlikely feat. Maurice now confesses that he is a humble tailor, not a noble baron.

News of Maurice's lowly social status spreads swiftly throughout the chateau through another traveling song with choruses sung by the Duke and the servants (Butler, Valet, Chambermaid, Chef, and Laundress) (**"The**

Son-of-a-Gun Is Nothing but a Tailor"). To the orchestral strains of "Love Me Tonight" Maurice leaves the chateau on foot to catch a train back to Paris as Jeanette realizes that her love for Maurice has enabled her to accept Maurice's lowly social position. Jeanette gets on her horse, catches up with Maurice's train, pledges her love, and risks her life by standing directly in the train's path and forcing it to stop. The Aunts, who have been weaving a tapestry in which a knight rescues a princess, have the last words, which have already served as the epigraph to this summary: "Once upon a time there was a Princess and a Prince Charming . . . Who was not a Prince. But who was charming. And they lived happily ever after . . ." (see Plot Figure 1, Plot Figure 2, and Plot Figure 3).

Plot Figure 1 The Three Aunts completing the tapestry of the Prince rescuing the Princess.
"And they lived happily ever after . . ."
Elizabeth Patterson (First Aunt) [left]
Blanche Friderici (Third Aunt) [center]
Ethel Griffies (Second Aunt) [right]

Plot Figure 2 The completed tapestry of the Prince rescuing the Princess.

Plot Figure 3 "The End" title over the completed tapestry of the Prince rescuing the Princess.

Sources

Library Collections and Film Studio Archives

Library Collections

Rouben Mamoulian Collection, Library of Congress, Washington, DC.
The Richard Rodgers Collection, Library of Congress, Washington, DC.
Production Code Files, Correspondence 1931–1954, Margaret Herrick Library, Los Angeles.
Richard Rodgers Papers 1914–1989, New York Public Library.

Paramount Archives, Music Archive, Paramount Pictures

Rodgers's handwritten scores
Conductor's Score
Love Me Tonight (Paramount), released August 19, 1932: Screenplay, Video and Audio Recordings, Lyrics, Scores.

Screenplay

Screenplay by Samuel Hoffenstein, Waldemar Young, and George Marion Jr.
Academy of Motion Picture Arts and Sciences (Core and Special Collections), Margaret Herrick Library, Los Angeles.

Video Recording

Love Me Tonight, Kino Video, K322 DVD (2003).

Audio Recordings

CD *The Ultimate Rodgers & Hart*—Volume I, Pearl Gem 0110, Pavilion
Records (2001). Maurice Chevalier and Jeanette MacDonald, with
Paramount Studio Orchestra conducted by Nat Finston, recorded
in 1932.
["The Poor Apache" (Chevalier); "Love Me Tonight" (MacDonald);
"Mimi" (Chevalier); "Isn't It Romantic?" (MacDonald)].

LP *Maurice Chevalier and Jeanette MacDonald: Three Classic Movie
Musicals* (Soundtrack Highlights). *The Love Parade, One Hour with
You,* and *Love Me Tonight,* Ariel Records, Ariel CMF 23 (n.d.) [recorded
in 1932].
Love Me Tonight songs: "That's the Song of Paree" (Chevalier et al.);
"Isn't It Romantic?" (Chevalier, Bert Roach, Rolf Sedan, Tyler Brooke,
soldiers, gypsies, MacDonald); "Lover" (MacDonald); "Mimi"
(Chevalier); "A Woman Needs Something Like That" (MacDonald
and Joseph Cawthorn); "The Poor Apache" (Chevalier); "Love Me
Tonight" (Chevalier and MacDonald).

Lyrics

Hart, Dorothy, and Robert Kimball, eds. *The Complete Lyrics of Lorenz
Hart.* New York: Knopf, 1985; expanded ed. New York: Da Capo, 1995.

Published Vocal Scores

Rodgers and Hart: A Musical Anthology. Milwaukee, WI: Hal Leonard,
1995. [piano-vocal sheet music] ["Isn't It Romantic?" "Love Me
Tonight," "Lover," and "Mimi"]; Famous Music Corporation [piano-
vocal sheet music].

DRAMATIS PERSONAE

The selected credits here for the cast of Love Me Tonight *Includes all films directed by Rouben Mamoulian, Ernst Lubitsch, and other selected films (mainly musical films). Arranged alphabetically with the major characters in capital letters.*[1]

Tyler Brooke (1886–1943); Composer

Appeared in 92 films between 1915 and 1943.
  Lubitsch: *Monte Carlo* (1930); *Trouble in Paradise* (1932); *The Merry Widow* (1934)
  Other films: *Hallelujah, I'm a Bum*, songs by Rodgers and Hart (1933)

Marion "Peanuts" Byron (1911–1985); Bakery Girl

After co-starring with Buster Keaton in *Steamboat Bill Jr.* (1928) played mainly brief roles, often uncredited, until 1938.

CHARLES BUTTERWORTH (1896–1946): Count de Savignac

Featured in nearly 50 films between 1929 and 1944 before his death in an automobile accident.
  Films: *The Cat and the Fiddle* (1934); *Hollywood Party*, songs by Rodgers and Hart (1934); *The Boys from Syracuse*, songs by Rodgers and Hart (1940); *This Is the Army* (1943)

Joseph Cawthorn (1868–1949): Dr. Armand de Pontignac

Appeared on Broadway from the late 1890s until 1927, then moved to Hollywood where he appeared in more than 50 films, including *Gold Diggers of 1935* and *The Great Ziegfeld* (1936).

MAURICE CHEVALIER (1888–1972): Maurice Courtelin

The film musical's first megastar, 1929–34, including 4 films with MacDonald.
  Lubitsch: *The Love Parade* (1929); *Paramount on Parade* (1930); *The Smiling Lieutenant* (1931); *One Hour with You* (1931); *The Merry Widow* (1934)
  Other films: *Love in the Afternoon* (1957); *Gigi* (1958); *Can-Can* (1960); *Fanny* (1961); *The Aristocats* (1970)

Cecil Cunningham (1888–1959): Laundress

Appeared in more than 80 films between 1929 and 1946.
  Lubitsch: *Paramount on Parade* (1930); *If I Had a Million* (1933)
  Mamoulian: *We Live Again* (1933)
  Other films: *People Will Talk* (1935); *The Awful Truth* (1937); *I Married an Angel*, songs by Rodgers and Hart (1942)

George Davis (1889–1965): Pierre

Appeared in nearly 300 films between 1916 and 1963, mostly uncredited, including two directed by Lubitsch.
  Lubitsch: *The Merry Widow* (1934); *Ninotchka* (1939)

Mary Doran (1910–1995): Mme. Dupont

Appeared in 80 films between 1927 and 1944.

Blanche Friderici (1878–1933): Third Aunt

Appeared in 60 films between 1920 and 1934, including *Flying Down to Rio* (1933) and *It Happened One Night* (1934).

Robert Greig (1879–1958): Major Domo Flamand

Best known for his roles as butler. Appeared in more than 100 films between 1930 and 1949.
  Lubitsch: *Trouble in Paradise* (1932)
  Other films: *Animal Crackers* (1930); *Horse Feathers* (1932); *Rose Marie* (1936); *The Great Ziegfeld* (1936); *The Lady Eve* (1941); *Sullivan's Travels* (1941); *The Palm Beach Story* (1942); *Unfaithfully Yours* (1948)

Ethel Griffies (1878–1975): Second Aunt

Appeared in scores of films between 1917 and 1965.
  Mamoulian: *We Live Again* (1934)
  Other films: *The Birds* (1963)

George "Gabby" Hayes (1885–1969): Grocer

Attributed with 193 acting credits from 1929 to 1950. Best known for Westerns. After completing his film career he starred in *The Gabby Hayes Show* television series, 1950–54 and 1956.

Mel Kalish (birth and death dates unknown): Chef

Six credits listed on IMDb between 1932 and 1939, including *Alexander's Ragtime Band* (1938).

MYRNA LOY (1905–1993): Countess Valentine

Featured in scores of films between 1925 and 1980, including 14 with William Powell
   Films: *The Jazz Singer* (1927), *The Thin Man* (1934) and six other *Thin Man* films, 1936–1947; *The Great Ziegfeld* (1936); *The Best Years of Our Lives* (1946); *Mr. Blandings Builds His Dream House* (1948); *Cheaper by the Dozen* (1950)

JEANETTE MACDONALD (1903–1965): Princess Jeanette

Starred in 4 films with Chevalier (1929–32), 8 films with Nelson Eddy (1934–42), and 17 other films in the 1930s and 1940s.
   Lubitsch: *The Love Parade* (1929); *Monte Carlo* (1930); *One Hour with You* (1931); *The Merry Widow* (1934)
   Other films: *The Cat and the Fiddle* (1934); *Naughty Marietta* (1935); *Rose Marie* (1936); *San Francisco* (1936); *Maytime* (1937); *The Firefly* (1937); *The Girl of the Golden West* (1937); *Sweethearts* (1938); *New Moon* (1940); *Bitter Sweet* (1940): *I Married an Angel*, songs by Rodgers and Hart (1942)

Tony Merlo (1886–1976): Hatmaker

Appeared in 84 films between 1916 and 1950.
   Lubitsch: *Desire* (1936)
   Other films: *Hallelujah, I'm a Bum*, songs by Rodgers and Hart; *Till the Clouds Roll By* (1946)

Edgar Norton (1869–1953): Valet

Appeared in more than 90 films between 1916 and 1948, including the memorable role of Dr. Jekyll's butler Poole in *Dr. Jekyll and Mr. Hyde*, directed by Mamoulian, the acclaimed horror film that directly preceded *Love Me Tonight.*
   Mamoulian: *Dr. Jekyll and Mr. Hyde* (1931); *We Live Again* (1933); *Rings on Her Fingers* (1942)
   Lubitsch: *Monte Carlo* (1930)

Rita Owin (1904–1979): Chambermaid

Twenty-three credits between 1932 and 1942.

Elizabeth Patterson (1874–1966): First Aunt

Appeared in dozens of films between 1926 at the age of fifty-one and 1960 when she was eighty-six.
Mamoulian: *High, Wide and Handsome* (1937)
Lubitsch: *Bluebeard's Eighth Wife* (1938)
Other films and television: *Little Woman* (1949); *I Love Lucy*, television series, eleven episodes (1952–56); *Pal Joey*, songs by Rodgers and Hart (1957)

Thomas Ricketts (1853–1939): Rochambeau (Man in Photo)

The first Ebenezer Scrooge in a filmed version of *A Christmas Carol* (1908). Also a director of many silent films.
Lubitsch: *If I Had a Million* (1932); *Bluebeard's Eighth Wife* (1938)
Other films: *It Happened One Night* (1934); *Top Hat* (1935); *Show Boat* (1936); *Gold Diggers of 1937* (1936); *A Star Is Born* (1937)

Bert Roach (1891–1971): Emile

Appeared in 327 films between 1914 and 1951 (according to Wikipedia), including *No, No, Nanette* (1930); *Hallelujah, I'm a Bum*, songs by Rodgers and Hart (1933); *San Francisco* (1936)

CHARLIE RUGGLES (1886–1970): Gilbert, Vicomte de Varèze

Appeared in nearly 100 films between 1929 and 1966.
Lubitsch: *The Smiling Lieutenant* (1931); *One Hour with You* (1932); *Trouble in Paradise* (1932); *If I Had a Million* (1932)
Other films and television: *Ruggles of Red Gap* (1935); *People Will Talk* (1935); *Anything Goes* (1936); *Bringing Up Baby* (1938); *The Parent Trap* (1961); *The Pleasure of His Company* (1961); *Papa's Delicate Condition* (1963); *Bewitched*, television series, two episodes (1964–65); *The Beverly Hillbillies*, television series, three episodes (1965–66)

Rolfe Sedan (1897–1982): Taxi Driver

Appeared in many films between 1921 and 1979, mostly uncredited.
Mamoulian: *High, Wide and Handsome* (1937); *Silk Stockings* (1957)
Lubitsch: *Paramount on Parade* (1930); *Monte Carlo* (1930); *Trouble in Paradise* (1932); *Design for Living* (1933); *The Merry Widow* (1934); *Bluebeard's Eighth Wife* (1938); *Ninotchka* (1939)
Other films: *42nd Street* (1933); *The Cat the Fiddle* (1934); *The Thin Man* (1934); *Ruggles of Red Gap* (1935); *Rose Marie* (1936); *Anything Goes* (1936); *Shall We Dance* (1937); *The Firefly* (1937); *The Wizard of Oz* (1939); *The Story of Vernon and Irene Castle* (1939); *April in Paris* (1952); *Gentlemen Prefer Blondes* (1953)

C. Aubrey Smith (1863–1948): Duke D'Artelines

Appeared in scores of films between 1915 and 1949.
  Mamoulian: *Queen Christina* (1933)
  Lubitsch: *Trouble in Paradise* (1932); *Cluny Brown* (1946)
  Other films: *Rebecca* (1940); *Little Women* (1949)

William H. Turner (1861–1942): Bootmaker

Eighty-five credits between 1913 and 1936, mainly in silent films.

Ethel Wales (1878–1952): Dressmaker (Mme. Dutoit)

Appeared in 138 films between 1920 and 1950, mostly uncredited. In the cast list provided in the 2003 DVD Kino K322, Wales's birth date is listed as 1898. This erroneous
  date explains why Miles Kreuger stated in his entertaining and informative Audio
  Commentary that although she looked much older, Wales was only thirty-four years
  old. In fact, she was fifty-four at the time.

Gordon Westcott (1903–1935): Credit Manager

Appeared in 38 films between 1928 and 1935, nearly all credited, including *Footlight
  Parade* (1933).

Clarence Wilson (1876–1941): Shirtmaker

Appeared in nearly 200 films between 1920 and 1941.
  Films: *The Front Page* (1931); *Hollywood Party*, songs by Rodgers and Hart; *Ruggles of
Red Gap* (1935); *A Star Is Born* (1937); *You Can't Take It with You* (1938)

MUSICAL CONTENTS AND TIMINGS

0:31 **Prelude (C to F major) (instrumental), Title and Credits**
Main Title (Street Music [whole-tone melody]) (0:42)
Myrna's Theme (0:49)
Duke Theme (with fanfare) (1:05)
Aunts Theme (1:14)
Camera Theme (1:25)
Street Scene Tune (whole-tone melody) (1:34)

1:42 **"Symphony of Noises" (street sounds)**
Gershwin: "Wintergreen for President" from *Of Thee I Sing* (1931) (3:48; 3:53)

3:58 "Street Scene" (instrumental)
Street Scene Tune
Gershwin: "Wintergreen for President" (4:08; 4:12; 4:13; 4:15; 4:40)

4:43 **"The Song of Paree" (D to C major) (Maurice, Duval, First Girl, Second Girl, Woman in Window, Bakery Girl, Mrs. Bendix, Grocer, Girl, Young Fellow, Man in Window, Café Man, M. Cohen)**
Street Scene Tune (instrumental) (4:43)
"It's not a sonata by Mozart" (4:57)
Street Scene Tune (Instrumental) (5:28)
"It has taxi horns and klaxons" (instrumental) (5:31)
Street Scene Tune (instrumental) (5:58)
"Bonjour Duval" (mostly spoken, melody in orchestra) (6:12)

7:28 "How Are You Interlude" (based on the "Bonjour Duval" melody) (instrumental)

8:41 Ruggles Theme (instrumental)

11:19 Mendelssohn: "Wedding March" from *A Midsummer Night's Dream* (1826) (in triple meter) (instrumental)

11:52 **"Isn't It Romantic?" (E-flat to F-sharp major, actual pitch) (Maurice, Emile, Taxi Driver, Composer, Soldiers, Gypsy (Roma] Violinist, Jeanette)**
Verse: "My face is glowing" (11:52) (E-flat major)
Chorus: "Isn't It Romantic?" (12:21)
Emile (13:13)
Taxi Driver (14:03)
Composer (on train) (14:27)
Soldiers (14:52) [F-sharp major]
Gypsy Violinist (15:20) (with shadows)
Jeanette (16:05)

18:50 Camera Theme (instrumental), entering the Aunts' tower with their shadows cast on the wall

19:09 Aunts Theme (instrumental)

19:38 Camera Theme (instrumental), entering the Aunts' tower with their shadows cast on the wall

19:58 Duke Theme (instrumental)

20:28   Butler Theme (instrumental)

21:16   Metz and Hayden: "There'll Be a Hot Time in the Old Town Tonight" ("a la dirge") (1896) (instrumental)

21:44   Ruggles Theme (instrumental)

23:27   Aunts Theme (instrumental)

23:54   "Isn't It Romantic?" (instrumental), Jeanette sleeping 24:29 "Paris Roofs" (same as Street Scene Tune)

26:04   Ladré and Bécourt: "Ça Ira" ("It'll Be Fine") (1790) (underscoring)

27:40   "Lover" (Jeanette)

30:34   "Mimi" (Maurice)

32:57   "Happy Mimi" (based on "Mimi") (instrumental)

34:19   Ruggles Theme (instrumental)

34:58   "A Woman Needs Something Like That" (Dr. Armond de Pontignac, Jeanette)[1]

Doctor: "And now, my dear, remove your dress" [spoken] (34:58)

Jeanette: "I feel depressed when I'm alone in bed at night" [sung: 11 seconds] (36:11)

Mendelssohn: "Spring Song," Op. 62/6 from *Songs without Words* (1842–44) (36:49)

Jeanette: "Sweet music makes me cry and pout" [sung: 11 seconds] (37:16)

Jeanette: "I'm wasting away" [sung: 8 seconds] (37:32)

39:36   "Ça Ira" (first eight measures) (instrumental) (Maurice arrives outside the chateau)

39:53   Mozart: "Minuet" from the act I Finale of *Don Giovanni* (instrumental) (Maurice enters the hallway of the chateau)

40:16   "March Maestoso" (based on the Monsieur Duval melody and "How Are You?") (Maurice explores the interior of the chateau with every moment in the music synchronized to Maurice's movements) (instrumental)

41:28   Gilbert and Sullivan: "Hail, Hail, the Gang's All Here" from *The Pirates of Penzance* (1879) (Maurice descends the chateau stairs and sees the residents, i.e., the "gang") (instrumental)

41:42   "Hail, Hail" (piccolo solo of the second phrase)

41:47   "A la Intermezzo" (underscoring)

42:03   Butler Theme (instrumental)

42:08   "Isn't It Romantic?" (instrumental)

42:27   Aunt's Theme (underscoring)

43:00   "Isn't It Romantic?" (instrumental)

43:07   Duke Theme (instrumental)

45:00   Aunts Theme (instrumental)

45:30   "Mimi" (instrumental)

45:59   Bird Calls (no tune)

46:00   "Mimi" (reprise) (Duke D'Artelines, Gilbert, Second and First Aunt, Count de Savignac)

The Duke (46:16)

Myrna [filmed but removed before the rerelease in 1949]

Gilbert (46:51)

Aunts (47:20)

Count (47:47)

48:14 Horn Solo (the Count's horn dissolves into a horn held by a man on horseback who announces the hunt)

52:22 The Hunt
Horns (52:22)
Deer (52:47) (flute cadenza); Dogs (52:50)
Deer (52:57) (rhythm, pizzicato articulation, and several pitches based on the opening
of the "Pizzicato" movement from Delibes's *Sylvia* [1876])
Dogs (53:02); Deer (53:05) (Delibes allusion)
Dogs (53:10); Deer (53:15) (Delibes allusion)
Dogs (53:18); Deer (53:24) (Delibes allusion)
Dogs (53:25); Deer (53:30) (Delibes allusion)
Dogs (53:32); Deer (53:35) (rhythm of the conclusion of Delibes's "Pizzicato" movement)
Dogs (53:39)
Horns (54:01)
Duke (laughs) (57:15): "Go back quickly and quietly, on tiptoes" (underscoring)
End of "The Hunt" (57:45)

59:00 The Ball (instrumental underscoring)
Johann Strauss Jr.: *Thousand and One Nights*, Op. 346 (1871)

62:00 "The Poor Apache" (Maurice) (with Maurice's shadow on the wall)

65:15 "Lover" (underscoring)

65:39 "Scherzo" (underscoring)

67:11 "Appassionato (Voluptuously)" (after "she kisses him") (underscoring)

67:18 Jeanette: "How foolish I was" (underscoring)

67:48 "Isn't It Romantic?" (underscoring)

69:43 "Love Me Tonight Waltz" (instrumental)

70:32 Camera Theme (instrumental), the first and only time the camera enters Maurice's bedroom, not the Aunts' tower

71:15 "Love Me Tonight" (Jeanette and Maurice)

74:30 "More Help" (instrumental)

75:14 Duke Theme (instrumental)

76:43 **"Isn't It Romantic?" (reprise) (Maurice humming while measuring Jeanette for her riding habit)**

80:58 **"The Son-of-a-Gun Is Nothing but a Tailor" (Duke, First and Second Aunt, Count, Picture of D'Artelines Ancestor, Major Domo Flamand, Valet, Chambermaid, Chef, Laundress, Jeanette, Men's Chorus)**
Duke (80:58); Butler (81:51)
Valet (82:04); Chambermaid (82:21)
Chef (82:36); Laundress (82:51)
Jeanette (spoken) (83:17)

84:37 **"Love Me Tonight" (reprise) (one chorus: AA Maurice; BA Jeanette)**

85:36 "Love Me Tonight" (instrumental reprise and underscoring at a lively tempo)
AABA A and five additional AABA choruses with a *ritardando* on the final A

88:29 Aunts Theme ("Once upon a time there was a Princess and a Prince Charming) (underscoring)

89:59 End of film

SONGS AND MAJOR INSTRUMENTAL NUMBERS

Prelude (C to F major) (instrumental) (Film 0:00–1:41)

a) Rodgers's handwritten score (Paramount)
b) Conductor's Score (Paramount, July 29, 1932) (C to F major)

"Symphony of Noises" (street sounds) (Film 1:42–3:57)
"The Song of Paree" (Maurice, Duval, First Girl, Second Girl, Woman in Window, Bakery Girl, Mrs. Bendix, Grocer, Girl, Young Fellow, Man in Window, Café Man, M. Cohen) (Film 4:43–7:26)

a) Rodgers's Vocal Score (lyrics included) (LOC, Box 10, Folder 24) (D major to C major)
b) Conductor's Score (Paramount, January 21, 1932) (D major to C major)
c) Film (D major to C major)
d) LP (D major to C major)

"Isn't It Romantic?" (Maurice, Emile, Taxi Driver, Composer, Soldiers, Gypsy Violinist, Jeanette) (Film 11:52–17:32)

a) Rodgers's Vocal Score (with partial lyrics) (LOC Box 10, Folder 16) (D major to F major)
b) Conductor's Score (Paramount, May 11, 1932) (D major to F major)
c) Film (E-flat major to F-sharp major)
d) LP (E-flat major to F-sharp major)
e) Published Vocal Score (1) (E-Flat major)
f) CD of 1932 commercial recording: Jeanette MacDonald (E major)

"Lover" (Jeanette) (Film 27:40–28:56)

a) Rodgers's Vocal Score (no lyrics) (LOC, Box 10, Folder 18) (D major)
b) Conductor's Score (Paramount, April 21, 1932) (D major)
c) Film (D major)
d) LP (D major)
e) Published Vocal Score (1) (C major)

"Mimi" (Maurice) (Film 30:34–31:46)

a) Rodgers's Vocal Score (no lyrics) (LOC, Box 10, Folder 20) (G major)
b) Conductor's Score (Paramount, March 11, 1932) (G major)
c) Film (G major)
d) LP (A-flat major)
e) Published Vocal Score (1) (G major)
f) CD of 1932 commercial recording: Maurice Chevalier (G major)

"A Woman Needs Something Like That" (Dr. Armond de Pontignac, Jeanette) (Film 34:58–37:57)

a) Rodgers's Vocal Score (includes lyrics) (LOC, Box 10, Folder 25) (A minor–C major–F major)
b) Conductor's Score (Paramount, March 1, 1932) (A minor–C major–F major)
c) Film (A minor–C major–F major)
d) LP (A-flat minor–B major–F-sharp major)

"Mimi" (reprise) (Duke D'Artelines, Gilbert, Second and First Aunt, Count de Savignac) (Film 46:00–48:15)

a) Conductor's Score (Paramount, July 27, 1932) (G major) [includes Valentine's chorus]
b) Film (G major) [Valentine's chorus deleted]

The Hunt (Film 52:20–54:40)

a) Rodgers's handwritten score (Paramount) (D major to F major)
b) Conductor's Score (Paramount, July 29, 1932) (D major to F major)
c) Film (D major to F major)

"The Poor Apache" (Maurice) (Film 62:00–65:12)

a) Rodgers's Vocal Score (no lyrics) (LOC, Box 10, Folder 22) (verse B minor; chorus G major)
b) Conductor's Score (Paramount, April 17, 1932) (verse B minor; chorus G major)
c) Film (verse B minor; chorus G major)
d) LP (verse C minor; chorus A-flat major)
e) Published Vocal Score (2) (verse D minor; chorus B-flat major)
f) CD of 1932 commercial recording: Maurice Chevalier (verse B minor; chorus G major)

"Love Me Tonight" (Jeanette and Maurice) (Film 71:15–72:17)

a) Rodgers's Vocal Score (no lyrics) (LOC, Box 10, Folder 17) (D major)
b) Conductor's Score (Paramount, March 7, 1932) (D major)
c) Film (D major)
d) LP (E-flat major)
e) Published Vocal Score (1) (F major)
f) CD of 1932 commercial recording: Jeanette MacDonald (D major)

"Isn't It Romantic?" (reprise) (Maurice humming while measuring Jeanette for her riding habit) (Film 76:43–77:45)

a) Film (D major)

"The Son-of-a-Gun Is Nothing but a Tailor" (Duke, First and Second Aunt, Count, Picture of D'Artelines Ancestor, Major Domo Flamand, Valet, Chambermaid, Chef, Laundress, Jeanette, Men's Chorus) (Film 80:58–83:13)

a) Rodgers's Vocal score (no lyrics) (LOC, Box 10, Folder 23) (D major)
b) Conductor's Score (Paramount, February 16, 1932) (D major)
c) Film (D major)

"Love Me Tonight" (reprise) (one chorus: AA Maurice; BA Jeanette) (Film 83:37–85:32)

a) Film (D major)

"Love Me Tonight" (instrumental reprise and underscoring at a lively tempo) (Film 85:36–88:10)
AABA A and five additional AABA choruses with a *ritardando* on the final A

a) Film (F major)

Notes

Series Editor's Foreword

1. "Para's 'Love Me Tonight' Certain Smash Anywhere: Every Department of Production Fine," *Hollywood Reporter*, August 5, 1932, 2.
2. Geoffrey Block, *Enchanted Evenings: The Broadway Musical from "Show Boat" to Sondheim and Lloyd Webber* (New York: Oxford University Press, 1997; rev. ed., 2009); Geoffrey Block, *Richard Rodgers* (New Haven, CT: Yale University Press, 2003); Geoffrey Block, *The Richard Rodgers Reader* (New York: Oxford University Press, 2002).
3. Richard Rodgers, *Musical Stages: An Autobiography* (New York: Random House, 1975), 148.

Preface

1. Geoffrey Block, *Richard Rodgers* (New Haven, CT: Yale University Press, 2003).
2. The name "passed-along song" was coined by Jane Feuer in the original 1982 edition of *The Hollywood Musical* (Bloomington: Indiana University Press, 1982; expanded ed. 1993), 16 of both editions. Rouben Mamoulian used the term "traveling song." Mamoulian, "The History of the Motion Picture," 48, Rouben Mamoulian Collection, Library of Congress, Box 198, Folder 5.
3. Richard Rodgers, *Musical Stages: An Autobiography* (New York: Random House, 1975), 148–53.
4. *Love Me Tonight* was not the first full Rodgers and Hart film score. The previous year they had contributed three songs to *The Hot Heiress* (March 1931). Before returning to Broadway with *Jumbo* in November 1935 they would also compose the songs for *The Phantom President* starring George M. Cohan (September 1932), *Hallelujah, I'm a Bum* starring Al Jolson (January 1933), *Hollywood Party* starring Jimmy Durante (May 1934), and *Mississippi* starring Bing Crosby (April 1935).
5. Leonard Maltin, *Turner Classic Movies Presents Leonard Maltin's Classic Movie Guide: From the Silent Era through 1965*, 3rd ed. (New York: Plume, 2015), 410. In *The Rough Guide to Film Musicals* (London: Penguin, 2007), a more concentrated survey, film critic and historian David Parkinson centers on a selected canon of "50 essential film musicals." Before discussing the films alphabetically, Parkinson shares his personal "Top Ten" list, in which *Love Me Tonight* gets the number three spot, directly following *Singin' in the Rain* and *Top Hat,* three steps ahead *The Wizard of Oz* (Parkinson, 76).
6. Jeanine Basinger, *The Movie Musical!* (New York: Knopf, 2019), 69.
7. *The Ultimate Rodgers and Hart Volume 1,* Pearl Gem 0110, Pavilion Records (2001).
8. Painted Smiles Records PSCD-106 (1989).
9. *Maurice Chevalier and Jeanette MacDonald: Three Classic Movie Musicals* (Soundtrack Highlights): *The Love Parade, One Hour with You,* and *Love Me Tonight,* Ariel Records, Ariel CMF 23 (n.d.). The only major song missing from this song list is "The-Son-of-a-Gun Is Nothing but a Tailor."
10. Andrew Sarris, *The American Cinema: Directors and Directions 1929–1968* (New York: Dutton, 1968; rev. ed., New York: Da Capo, 1996), 161; Sarris, "Lubitsch in the Thirties: All Talking! All Singing! All Lubitsch!" *Film Comment* 8, no. 2 (Summer 1972), 21.
11. Rodgers, *Musical Stages,* 148.
12. Hugh Fordin, *M-G-M's Greatest Musicals: The Arthur Freed Unit* (New York: Da Capo, 1996), 185.

Chapter 1: Introducing the Major Players and Developing the Screenplay for a Fairy Tale Musical

1. Rouben Mamoulian Collection, Library of Congress, White Script, Box 79, Folder 2, A-69 on page A-35.
2. Richard Rodgers, *Musical Stages: An Autobiography* (New York: Random House,1975), 148.
3. Hoffenstein (1890–1947) was the principal screenwriter for Mamoulian's previous film *Dr. Jekyll and Mr. Hyde* (1931) and would later contribute to the screenplays of *The Great Waltz* (1938), *The Wizard of Oz* (1939), *Laura* (1944), and Lubitsch's *Cluny Brown* (1946).
4. Young (1878–1938), the grandson of Brigham Young, wrote the screenplay to the film adaptation of *Sally* (1929) and a number of 1930s screenplays directed by Cecil B. De Mille.
5. Marion (1899–1968) wrote the screenplays to more than 100 films between 1920 and 1940 including *The Gay Divorcee* (1934). He also contributed the book for the original stage version of Rodgers and Hart's *Too Many Girls* (1939).
6. The German-born art director Dreier (1885–1966), originally recruited by fellow German Lubitsch to work on *Forbidden Paradise* in 1924, would go on to serve as the Art Director at Paramount for roughly 500 films from 1927 until he rode off into *Sunset Boulevard* (1950) and *A Place in the Sun* (1951). Among Dreier's films were four directed by Mamoulian: *Dr. Jekyll and Mr. Hyde* (1931), *Love Me Tonight* (1932), *Song of Songs* (1933), and *High, Wide and Handsome* (1937), the latter as co-art director. The same year as *Love Me Tonight,* Dreier also served as the art director for Lubitsch's *One Hour with You* and *Trouble in Paradise.*
7. Milner (1893–1972) was the cinematographer for 130 films from 1913 until his retirement in 1953. Although he also served as Mamoulian's cinematographer for *Song of Songs* one year after *Love Me Tonight,* Milner is mainly known today as Lubitsch's director of photography for the majority of his early sound films (1929–1936), including *The Love Parade, Monte Carlo, Paramount on Parade, Broken Lullaby, One Hour with You, Trouble in Paradise, Design for Living,* and *Desire.*
8. *Love Me Tonight* Production Code Files, Correspondence 1931–1954, Margaret Herrick Library, Los Angeles. As the director, Mamoulian was paid $28,000. Gary Marmorstein reports that Rodgers and Hart were paid $37,333.33 for *Love Me Tonight* and *The Phantom President* as a package. See Marmorstein, *A Ship without a Sail: The Life of Lorenz Hart* (New York: Simon & Schuster, 2012), 215.
9. Edwin M. Bradley in *The First Hollywood Musicals: A Critical Filmography of 171 Features, 1927 through 1932* (Jefferson, NC: McFarland, 1996), 35.
10. For information on Chevalier's life and career after he left Hollywood in the 1930s, including an explanatory discussion of the controversies surrounding his role in the French residence during Germany's occupation during World War II, see Edward Behr, *The Good Frenchman: The True Story of the Life and Times of Maurice Chevalier* (New York: Villard, 1993).
11. A total of twenty-eight actors and actresses were cast in *Love Me Tonight,* many in small roles and uncredited. Seven appeared in at least one other Mamoulian film and thirteen appeared in one or more films directed by Lubitsch, thus constituting something like a repertory company, one of the potential artistic strengths of the economically exploitative Hollywood studio system. See Appendix 1 for a complete cast list, including a guide to the cast members' appearances in other films directed by Mamoulian, Lubitsch, and selected films from throughout their often astoundingly prolific careers.
12. Despite her removal as a singer, the character of Valentine as played by Loy is so engaging that the *Time* magazine film critic quipped that the "the only illogicality is Chevalier's preferring Jeanette MacDonald to Myrna Loy." Anonymous, *Time,* August 29, 1932, quoted in Bradley, *The First Hollywood Musicals,* 310.
13. For a survey of Mamoulian's career on stage and film, see Mark Spergel, *Reinventing Reality: The Art and Life of Rouben Mamoulian* (Metuchen, NJ: Scarecrow, 1993); for a brief but insightful overview of the sixteen films see Tom Milne, *Mamoulian* (Bloomington: Indiana University Press, 1969), 1971).
14. Stage: George and Ira Gershwin (*Porgy and Bess,* 1935); Rodgers and Hammerstein (*Oklahoma!,* 1943, and *Carousel,* 1945); Duke and Dietz (*Sadie Thompson,* 1944); Arlen and Mercer (*St. Louis Woman,* 1946); Weill and Anderson (*Lost in the Stars,* 1949); Gould and Fields (*Arms and the Girl,* 1950). Film: Kern and Hammerstein (*High, Wide and Handsome,* 1937; Warren and Blaine (*Summer Holiday,* 1947); and Porter (*Silk Stockings,* 1957).
15. Mamoulian's lifetime honors include his induction into the Broadway Hall of Fame (1980) and the D. W. Griffith Award "for Lifetime Achievement." On Mamoulian's later years see Spergel,

Reinventing Reality, 215–37, and for more on Mamoulian's growing recognition see chapter 5 of this book, "The Reception of *Love Me Tonight* from Its Time to Ours."

16. Hugh Fordin, *M-G-M's Greatest Musicals: The Arthur Freed Unit* (New York: Da Capo, 1996), 185–86.

17. Spergel, *Reinventing Reality,* 2–3.

18. David Luhrssen, *Mamoulian: Life on Stage and Screen* (Lexington: University Press of Kentucky, 2013), 62.

19. See, for example, the interviews published in Charles Higham and Joel Greenberg, eds., *The Celluloid. Muse: Hollywood Directors Speak* (London: Angus and Robertson, 1969), 128–43; Andrew Sarris, ed., *Interviews with Film Directors* (Indianapolis, IN: Bobbs-Merrill, 1967), 286–92; and James R. Silke, ed., *Rouben Mamoulian: Style Is the Man* (Los Angeles: Center for Advanced Film Studies, 1971).

20. Spergel, *Reinventing Reality,* 33.

21. Ibid., 14.

22. Mamoulian, "The Psychology of Sound," Rouben Mamoulian Collection, Library of Congress, Box 139, Folder 10. Directly after this title Mamoulian clarified his agenda with the subtitle, "the second of a series of papers challenging the realistic conception of art"; "The History of the Motion Picture" is located in Box 182, Folder 3.

23. Mamoulian, "The History of the Motion Picture," 9.

24. Mamoulian, "The Psychology of Sound," 2.

25. Gene Ringgold and Dewitt Bodeen, *Chevalier: The Films and Career of Maurice Chevalier* (Secaucus, NJ: The Citadel, 1973), 110; reprinted in Spergel, *Reinventing Reality,* 135.

26. Patrick McGilligan, *George Cukor: A Double Life* (New York: St. Martin's, 1991), 69–72.

27. Ibid.

28. Ringgold and Bodeen, *Chevalier,* 110; reprinted in Spergel, *Reinventing Reality,* 135.

29. "To Aid in Chevalier Film: Leopold Marchand Is to Insure Authenticity of French Parts," *New York Times,* October 15, 1931, 26. Eventually Marchand would also get credit for the French adaptation of this film.

30. Ringgold and Bodeen, *Chevalier,* 110, 112; Spergel, *Reinventing Reality,* 135–36. Mamoulian and Marchand remained friends after the filming of *Love Me Tonight* and met frequently during Mamoulian's visit to Paris in September and October 1932. They even watched the release of the French version together on September 5. For those who wonder whether he ever met René Clair, the answer can be found in Mamoulian's contemporary diary which includes an entry for a meeting with the French director on September 8. Rouben Mamoulian Collection, Library of Congress, "Diaries and Diary Notes, 1932," Box 14, Folder 4.

31. Higham and Greenberg, *The Celluloid Muse,* 136.

32. Ibid.

33. Ibid.

34. Judith Thurman, *Secrets of the Flesh: A Life of Colette* (New York: Random House, 1999), 304.

35. *Catalog of Copyright Entries: Third Series,* 90. Act 1 (56 pages); Act 2 (63 pages); Act 3 (44 pages). *Le tailleur* was the second of four plays Marchand and Armont co-authored.

36. Rouben Mamoulian Collection, Library of Congress, "Synopsis," Box 78, Folder 1; Skeleton: Box 79, Folder 4. See table 1.1 for more details.

37. Rouben Mamoulian Collection, Library of Congress, "Treatment," Box 79, Folder 4; "Buff Script," Box 79, Folder 1; "White Script," Box 79, Folder 2.

38. A few samples of Rodgers and Hart songs from 1925 to 1930: "Here in My Arms" (*Dearest Enemy*); "Blue Room" (*The Girl Friend*); "Mountain Greenery" (*The Garrick Gaieties* of 1926*);* "My Heart Stood Still" and "Thou Swell" (*A Connecticut Yankee*); "You Took Advantage of Me" (*Present Arms*); "With a Song in My Heart" (*Spring Is Here*); "A Ship without a Sail" (*Head's Up!*); "Ten Cents a Dance" (*Simple Simon*); and "Dancing on the Ceiling" (*Ever Green*).

39. Rodgers, *Musical Stages,* 71.

40. Geoffrey Block, ed., *The Richard Rodgers Reader* (New York: Oxford University Press, 2002), 263.

41. Ethan Mordden, *Make Believe: The Broadway Musical in the 1920s* (New York: Oxford University Press, 1997), 118.

42. *Love Me Tonight,* Kino Video K322 DVD (2003).

43. Horowitz reports Paramount's original choice to commission an Oscar Straus score and a Samson Raphaelson screenplay without specifically mentioning *The Grand Duchess,* Hart biographer Gary Marmorstein mentions Raphaelson and the projected title by name but does not mention Straus, and neither Horowitz nor Marmorstein offers any corroborative sources. See

Horowitz, *"On My Way,"* 89, and Marmorstein, *A Ship without a Sail*, 201. The only source I have located that combines all these alleged facts is Kreuger's Audio Commentary to the 2003 DVD.

44. Ringgold and Bodeen, *Chevalier*, 110.

45. Upon their return in 1935 from their Hollywood Diaspora Rodgers and Hart would go on to create the shows for which they are best remembered, nine hits out of their ten shows between 1935 and Hart's death in 1943: *Jumbo; On Your Toes; Babes in Arms; I'd Rather Be Right; I Married an Angel; The Boys from Syracuse; Too Many Girls; Pal Joey;* and *By Jupiter.* For a survey of Rodgers and Hart's career from their first interpolated song on Broadway in 1919 to their departure for Hollywood in 1931 see Dominic Symonds, *We'll Have Manhattan: The Early Work of Rodgers and Hart* (New York: Oxford University Press, 2015). For a selective study of individual shows by Rodgers and Hart see Geoffrey Block, *Richard Rodgers* (New Haven, CT: Yale University Press, 2003) and *Enchanted Evenings: The Broadway Musical from "Show Boat" to Sondheim and Lloyd Webber* (New York: Oxford University Press, 1997; rev. 2nd ed., 2009). For useful surveys on Hart see Frederick Nolan, *Lorenz Hart* (New York: Oxford University Press, 1994) and Gary Marmorstein, *A Ship without a Sail.*

46. Rodgers, *Musical Stages*, 149.

47. Ibid.

48. Marmorstein, *A Ship without a Sail*, 202. Mamoulian noted in his calendar for 1931 that he had dinner with Rodgers on December 30, a meal preceded by successive lunches with Chevalier on December 23 and 24 and a dinner with Chevalier on December 29. Rouben Mamoulian Collection, Library of Congress, "Diaries and Diary Notes," Box 14, Folder 3.

49. *Love Me Tonight* Production Code Files, Correspondence 1931–1954, Margaret Herrick Library, Los Angeles.

50. Ibid.

51. Ibid., 149.

52. Ringgold and Bodeen, *Chevalier*, 112. This portion of Mamoulian's recollection was omitted in Spergel's *Reinventing Reality*, which instead includes an ellipsis after the first sentence and then proceeds to discuss Chevalier's attempt to take part in story conferences as he did with Lubitsch. Not only did Mamoulian explain that before these conferences he "was first working with the song writers," he emphatically wanted to exclude the star when the conferences did take place. When Chevalier threatened to complain to the front office, Mamoulian encouraged him to do so since he "hadn't wanted this picture and was only doing it as a favor to Mr. Zukor, and would consider it a very special favor if he could get me taken off it" (Spergel, 112). Mamoulian concludes this story by stating that Chevalier did not follow through on his threat and the two "remained close friends" until Chevalier's death in 1972.

53. Despite a considerably altered narrative, the Synopsis retains a number of essential plot points found in Marchand and Armont's play. In both, a tailor, Adolphe Hortigan in the play (Maurice in future treatments and screenplays), travels to the chateau where Gilbert de Varèze resides to collect the money due him for Gilbert's many unpaid suits. At the chateau in both, Maurice meets Nady de Pontbrisson (later Jeanette), whose father is the cousin to the Duke. Also in both, Adolphe/Maurice helps Nady with her arithmetic, falls in love with her, makes her a chic riding habit, and leaves without revealing his occupation. In contrast to the Synopsis (and future versions) the play *begins* at the chateau and remains there for the first two acts. Only in the final act does the play move to Hortigan's shop with its British-sounding name "Douglas and Craig." Here the tailor reveals the truth of his humble profession, and the play and Synopsis come to their respective happy resolution.

54. Jane Feuer, *The Hollywood Musical*, 2nd ed. (Bloomington: Indiana University Press, 1993), 16. Feuer introduced the term in the first edition in 1982, also on 16.

55. "The History of the Motion Picture" (December 6, 1939), Rouben Mamoulian Collection, Library of Congress, Box 182, Folder 3, 49.

56. Charlie Ruggles, Baron Gilbert de Varèze in the play, was designated *Vicomte* [Viscount] Gilbert de Varèze in the film, and Maurice became the Baron Courtelin.

57. When Hortigan tells Nady in the play on page 158 (out of 167 pages) that he is a tailor, Nady responds that she doesn't believe him. Not until two pages later does she grasp what Hortigan calls "la triste erité" ("the sad truth").

58. The deus ex machina (roughly "god from the machine") was a contrived plot device used in Greek and Roman theater, in which a godlike power unexpectedly swoops over the plot to save an otherwise hopeless situation.

59. Roland Young, the off-screen name for the popular actor who was projected for the role of the Baron before being replaced by Charles Butterworth (and renamed the Count de Savignac), had been recently featured in *One Hour with You* as Professor Oliver. He is best known for his starring titular role in *Topper* in 1937.

60. The Skeleton indicates its preference to cast Mitzi with Mitzi Green, then just under twelve. Although her character will disappear from the film prior to the Buff Script, Mitzi Green would return to the stage a few years later to star in Rodgers and Hart's *Babes in Arms* (1937), where she sang two of the show's biggest hits, "My Funny Valentine" and "The Lady Is a Tramp."

61. Known as the Wise, Charles V reigned from 1364 to 1380.

62. In future drafts the screenwriters continued to cultivate the idea of incorporating a sudden loud noise. In the course of the "passed-along" or "traveling" song, "The Son-of-a-Gun Is Nothing but a Tailor" in the White Script, the camera shifts to the temperamental and volatile horse Solitude who joins the derision of Maurice's exposure by kicking down a side of his stall, an action that creates "a terrific crash of timber." In the final film an even bigger noise occurs just before "The Son-of-a-Gun." This time the sound is created by the First Aunt (Elizabeth Patterson), who in her agitation at the revelation about Maurice inadvertently knocks over a vase, an action that creates an incongruously deafening cannon-like explosion to hilarious effect (see chapter 1 for a discussion of this explosion as an example of sonic stylization).

63. White Script: E-14; Release Script: Reel 8, page 4.

64. Mamoulian himself added these words and sent them in a telegram to Hoffenstein on April 4, 1932, asking him to place them at the end of the picture. Telegram from Mamoulian to Hoffenstein, April 4, 1932, Rouben Mamoulian Collection, "Correspondence Memoranda 1932–33," Box 77, Folder 8.

65. Rick Altman, *The American Film Musical* (Bloomington: Indiana University Press, 1987), 126.

66. Along with the "Isn't It Romantic?" montage, the "Symphony of Noises" is probably the most analyzed and discussed scene in the film. For more detail, including a consecutive "shot by shot" graphic illustration of the rhythmic and visual content from "Shot 5 high angle, street set workman enters" to "Shot 23 high angle street (as opening) street noises up, see Lea Jacobs, *Film Rhythm After Sound: Technology, Music, and Performance* (Oakland: University of California Press, 2015), 113–18 and chapter 3 of this volume. For more information on Mamoulian's earlier use of this technique in his role as the director of the stage play *Porgy* (1927), including a reprinting of the "Symphony of Noises" (Act 3, Scene 2), see Horowitz, "On My Way," 20–64 and 224–28.

67. Not only does she lose the opportunity to sing the central love song (or indeed anything at all beyond about fifteen seconds of the "Mimi" reprise), Valentine, like the Count, is gradually removed as a serious romantic alternative, a decision that reinforces the film's bona fides as a fairy tale musical: "Instead of pitting the lovers as a unit against an enemy who is ridiculous (from the Latin meaning 'laughable'), the fairy tale musical typically places an obstacle within each lover, in the form of pride or vanity." Altman, *The American Film Musical*, 144.

68. Rouben Mamoulian Collection, Library of Congress, Box 78, Folder 3, "Music & Lyrics (Lyrics 1932)." See Hannah Lewis, "*Love Me Tonight* (1932) and the Development of the Integrated Film Musical," *Musical Quarterly* 100, no. 1 (December 2017): 27. The lyrics to "Give Me Just a Moment" are also printed in *The Complete Lyrics of Lorenz Hart*, ed. Dorothy Hart and Robert Kimball (New York: Knopf, 1986; expanded ed. New York: Da Capo, 1995), 177. Although the assumption remains that Hart would not have written these lyrics in the absence of a Rodgers melody, the music to "Give Me Just a Moment" has not yet been located.

69. "Lover" is the only set of lyrics not mentioned in the extant production files in the Margaret Herrick Library. Its appearance in the White Script marks its first entry in the *Love Me Tonight* source material.

70. Altman, *The American Film Musical*, 157.

71. April 20, 1932, memo from Trotti to Jesse L. Lasky, *Love Me Tonight* Production Code Files, Correspondence 1931–1954, Margaret Herrick Library, Los Angeles. Trotti was the assistant to Colonel Jason S. Joy, Association of Motion Picture Producers and Distributors of America (MPPDA) from 1925 to 1932. The following year Trotti began a productive and distinguished career as a screenwriter, which included nominations for *Young Mr. Lincoln* (1939) and Irving Berlin's song cavalcade *There's No Business Like Show Business* (1954), earning the Best Original Screenplay Oscar for *Wilson* (1944). He also co-wrote the screenplay for the earlier Berlin song parade *Alexander's Ragtime Band* in 1938.

Chapter 2: Songs by Rodgers and Hart

1. William W. Appleton, ed., *Richard Rodgers: Letters to Dorothy 1926–1937* (New York: New York Public Library, 1988), 156.
2. Although not officially crowned, Rodgers deserves the title of "Waltz King" among the great (non-operetta) songwriters of his era. Nearly every show has one. The best-known, mainly composed for Broadway but also for Hollywood and television, include the following: 1930s— "Lover," "The Most Beautiful Girl in the World," and "Falling in Love with Love"; 1940s—"Oh, What a Beautiful Mornin'," "It's a Grand Night for Singing," "A Wonderful Guy," "This Nearly Was Mine": 1950s—"Hello Young Lovers," "Ten Minutes Ago," "My Favorite Things," and "Edelweiss"; 1960s—"Do I Hear a Waltz?"
3. Peggy Lee (vocal) with Gordon Jenkins and His Orchestra, recorded May 1, 1952 (Decca 28215); rereleased in the *Smithsonian Collection of Recordings, American Songbook Series: Rodgers/Hart* (Sony RD 048-6, A 22408) (1992). Decades later Bernadette Peters sang a similarly Latin-tinged duple version of another 1930s Rodgers and Hart waltz, "Falling in Love with Love" in the 1997 remake of *Cinderella.*
4. Don Tyler, *Hit Songs 1900–1955: American Popular Music of the Pre-Rock Era* (Jefferson, NC: McFarland, 2007), 189. According to Ted Gioia, Lee's version climbed up to No. 3 on the *Billboard* charts, matching the success of Paul Whiteman's recording of April 4, 1932, months before the film's release. Ted Gioia, *The Jazz Standards: A Guide to the Repertoire* (New York: Oxford University Press, 2012), 242. See note 58.
5. Although "Isn't It Romantic?" is often mentioned in the literature on Wilder and *Sabrina*, the presence of "Lover" as dance music for an evening party in the Hamptons in Wilder's film has seemingly gone unnoticed. Thanks to my copy-editor Joellyn Ausanka for pointing out that Wilder also used "Lover" in *The Major and the Minor.*
6. The song did not, however, make it to the soundtrack of the later film reincarnation of the song and film titled *Isn't It Romantic?* released in 2019.
7. *AFI's 100 Years . . . 100 Songs,* American Film Institute 2004, http://www.afi.com/100Years/Songs. aspx (accessed August 22, 2019). Rodgers was the most represented composer with six songs. The five with Oscar Hammerstein include one each from *The King and I* (# 54 "Shall We Dance") and *South Pacific* (#28 "Some Enchanted Evening"), and three from *The Sound of Music* (#10 "The Sound of Music," #64 "My Favorite Things," and "#88 Do-Re-Mi").
8. Alec Wilder, *American Popular Music: The Great Innovators, 1900–1950* (New York: Oxford University Press, 1972), 190–91. At the outset of his chapter on Rodgers, Wilder wrote, "Of all the writers whose songs are considered and examined in this book, those of Rodgers show the highest degree of consistent excellence, inventiveness, and sophistication" (163).
9. Allison Robbins, "Rescoring *Anything Goes* in 1930s Hollywood," in *The Oxford Handbook of Musical Theatre Screen Adaptations,* ed. Dominic McHugh (New York: Oxford University Press, 2019), Table 27.1, 619.
10. *The Rodgers and Hart Songbook* (New York: Simon & Schuster, 1951), 118–29; *Rodgers and Hart: A Musical Anthology* (Milwaukee: Hal Leonard, 1995), 189–203. The musical analysis in this chapter uses the keys of the published version for these four songs: "Isn't It Romantic," published in E-flat (same as the Conductor's Score, the film, and the 1932 recording); "Lover," published in C major (D major in the Conductor's Score); "Mimi," published in G major (A major in the Conductor's Score); "Love Me Tonight," published in F major (Conductor's Score and 1932 recording in D major). Since the published score of "The Poor Apache" (B-flat major) does not include the Trio, the present discussion will use the Conductor's Score (G major) as its point of reference.
11. In film parlance, diegetic (or actual) sound can also refer to a sound that originates on screen or off screen "capable of being heard by the real or fictive inhabitants of the filmed world, whether or not it was recorded during production." Bruce F. Kawin, *How Movies Work* (New York: Macmillan, 1987), 539. For an informative study of how it evolved that film, theater, opera, and musical theater and film scholars have succeeded in misinterpreting Aristotle's meaning of "diegesis" and "diegetic" and appropriated the new meaning for situations on the stage and film when "the characters of the story hear music," see Stefano Castelvecchi, "On 'Diegesis' and 'Diegetic': Words and Concepts," *Journal of the American Musicological Society* 73, no. 1 (Spring 2020); 149–71; quotation on 171. Since most theater and film scholars understand the way the term diegetic is used in this present volume (and since not even Castelvecchi has created a workable alternative), I stand by the word diegetic.

12. Mark N. Grant, *The Rise and Fall of the Broadway Musical* (Boston: Northeastern University Press, 2004), 239.

13. Highlights of the series include *Nobody Home* and *Very Good Eddie* (1915); *Oh, Boy!* and *Leave it to Jane* (1917); and *Oh, Lady! Lady!* (1918). Of these shows, all with music by Kern and a book by Bolton, only *Leave It to Jane* did not originate or play at the Princess.

14. Louis R. Reid, "Composing While You Wait," *Dramatic Mirror,* June 2, 1917, 5, quoted in Geoffrey Block, "Integration," *The Oxford Handbook of The American Musical,* ed. Raymond Knapp, Mitchell Morris, and Stacy Wolf (New York: Oxford University Press, 2011), 100.

15. On the central characteristics of the integrated musical, see Geoffrey Block, "Integration," in *The Oxford Handbook of the American Musical,* ed. Raymond Knapp, Mitchell Morris, and Stacy Wolf, 97–110 especially 98–99; reprinted in *Histories of the Musical: An Oxford Handbook of the American Musical, Volume 1,* ed. Knapp, Morris, and Wolf (New York: Oxford University Press, 2018), 153–75, especially 154–57. The idea of integration has been challenged, in Block's view unsuccessfully. For example, Scott McMillin argues that the division between spoken dialogue and song is fundamentally incompatible and precludes the integration of the two. See McMillin, *The Musical as Drama: A Study of the Principles and Conventions behind Musical Shows from Kern to Sondheim* (Princeton, NJ: Princeton University Press, 2006).

16. John Mueller, "Fred Astaire and the Integrated Musical," *Cinema Journal* 24, no. 1 (Fall 1984), 31.

17. Paramount Archives, Music Archives, Paramount Pictures. Thanks to Annie Killelea at Paramount for making these scores available to me.

18. The film version of this opening portion contains a rare lyric change, the substitution of "Yet thank God it's no Viennese waltz" with "But at least it's no Viennese waltz." The change was made in response to a January 28, 1932, request from the Studio Relations Committee upon receiving Hart's reference to God in his lyrics a few days earlier.

19. In *Musical Stages* Rodgers notes his use of "what was then called rhythmic dialogue," which he first used in *Love Me Tonight* and again in *The Phantom President* (1932) and *Hallelujah, I'm a Bum* (1933). Rodgers preferred the term "musical dialogue": "We simply used rhymed conversation, with musical accompaniment, to affect a smoother transition to actual song and to give the entire film a firmer musical structure." Rodgers, *Musical Stages,* 156. The next decade, now with Hammerstein but again with Mamoulian, the new team used rhythmic (or "musical") dialogue prominently and effectively at the beginning of the "Bench Scene" in *Carousel.*

20. We know that film was completed not long after the date on the "How Are You Interlude" manuscript pages from a memo dated August 8, 1932, to the administrators at the Studio Relations Committee, in which they note they had just seen "the new Chevalier picture, *Love Me Tonight.*"

21. Dorothy Hart and Robert Kimball, eds., *The Complete Lyrics of Lorenz Hart* (New York: Knopf, 1986; expanded ed. New York: Da Capo, 1995), 169.

22. *Ben Bagley's Everyone Else Revisited* (Painted Smiles PSCD-146) (1993). The singer is Dorothy Loudon. In the notes to the Appendix of the expanded edition of *The Complete Lyrics of Lorenz Hart* published by Da Capo Press in 1995 (327), Kimball announced that the refrain (chorus) had been located. See Mark Eden Horowitz, *Guides to Special Collections in the Music Division of the Library of Congress, The Richard Rodgers Collection* (Library of Congress, Washington, DC, 1995), Box 20, Folder 4, Miscellaneous Sketches [M.S. 6], 118.

23. After the first 8 bars of each A group, the music of the second 8 bars begins with the same phrase, which suggests an alternative interpretation of A-B-A-B.

24. The last words of the published song Do you mean that I will fall in love, perchance? Isn't it romance?" are the same in an intended reprise for Chevalier to sing at a later point in the film but not used. For a comparison between the film version and the published version see *The Complete Lyrics of Lorenz Hart,* 172–73.

25. The meaning and use of leitmotivs will be discussed in chapter 3.

26. It was noted in the previous chapter that as early as the Skeleton and again in the Treatment the projected screenplay at the time called for a scene in the chateau stables with Jeanette, Maurice, and her horse in "a song as yet untitled." The scene disappears in the Buff Script and returns in its final film context in the White Script.

27. Buff Script, D-52.

28. Edward Baron Turk, *Hollywood Diva: A Biography of Jeanette MacDonald* (Berkeley: University of California Press, 1998), 79. Turk later notes that after *Love Me Tonight* MacDonald "declared that her underwear days were over: 'I don't think my career of risqué roles has really hurt. I just feel I have gone far enough in lingerie. . . . I'm sure that people must say about me on the screen, 'Good gracious, is Jeanette MacDonald going to take off her clothes—*again*?' " (123).

29. Treatment of January 18, 1932, Sequence D, 14.
30. Buff Script, Sequence F, 36.
31. According to Hart and Kimball in *The Complete Lyrics of Lorenz Hart*, "The Poor Apache" was based on another song about Apache culture intended for Chevalier called "Cleaning Up the Floor with Lulu," 175–76 (lyrics included).
32. "Apaches (subculture)," https://en.wikipedia.org/wiki/Apaches_(subculture) (accessed August 28, 2019).
33. Spergel, *Reinventing Reality—The Art and Life of Rouben Mamoulian* (Metuchen, NJ: Scarecrow, 1993), 45
34. To this short list Mark Spergel adds the use of shadow-play in the bandit encampment in *The Gay Desperado* (1936). Spergel, *Reinventing Reality*, 133. Mamoulian's remarks about shadows in *The Gay Desperado* are applicable to use of this technique in "The Poor Apache" and in two scenes with the Aunts stirring their brew in their tower: "Shadows deepen your pictures, they add tremendously to the third dimension, and they enlarge the figures. They make them more important and impressive when you want them to be so." Rouben Mamoulian Collection, Library of Congress, "The History of the Motion Picture," 54, Box 198, Folder 5.
35. Rick Altman, *The American Film Musical* (Bloomington: Indiana University Press, 1989), 168.
36. Edwin M. Bradley, *The First Hollywood Musicals: A Critical Filmography of 171 Features, 1927 through 1932* (Jefferson, NC: McFarland, 1996), 256.
37. Lee Jacobs, "The Innovation of Re-Recording in the Hollywood Studios," *Film History* 24 (2012), 23.
38. Ibid.
39. Mamoulian used a metronome and often a baton in many of his pictures, including *Love Me Tonight*: "Most of *Love Me Tonight* was shot to a metronome. There is hardly a movement in that picture that was not done strictly in the music. This is why I think *Love Me Tonight* is a pure example of what a musical film should be, in my opinion." "The History of the Motion Picture," 53, Rouben Mamoulian Collection, Library of Congress, Box 198, Folder 5. Referring to his "Symphony of Noises" a little earlier in this essay Mamoulian acknowledged that he would "use a metronome quite frequently in pictures,—whenever precise and sustained timing is necessary for action or camera" and that "every noise in in that opening of *Love Me Tonight* was timed and rhythmically co-related with the beats of the metronome" (Ibid.).
40. Following the screening of *The Gay Desperado* as part of his lecture, "The History of the Motion Picture," Mamoulian was asked if the film was recorded. After stating unequivocally that "it was pre-recorded," he defended the practice: "You lose a great deal in the quality of singing and much time if you do it while you are shooting. Also, it is too complicated and the results are not as good" (52). Rouben Mamoulian Collection, Library of Congress, Box 198, Folder 5.
41. Miles Kreuger Audio Commentary, *Love Me Tonight*, Kino Video, K322 DVD (2003).
42. Perhaps based on his conversations with Kreuger, in turn based on Kreuger's conversations with Rodgers, Joseph Horowitz argues that the singers were recorded on the set: "Mamoulian recorded the orchestral soundtrack before he filmed his singing actors: what we see and hear is therefore the actual singing. That is, music creates the conditions for words, not the other way around. Even more important: Chevalier and MacDonald can sing and act more expressively than if they were mouthing songs they had already dubbed." Horowitz, "On My Way," 93.
43. Mamoulian, "The History of the Motion Picture," 45. Rouben Mamoulian Collection, Library of Congress, Box 198, Folder 5. Included in the Gallery of Photos, one of the Supplemental Features of the KINO DVD of *Love Me Tonight* is a filming shot of "The Song of Paree" where it is possible to see the cylinder used for on set recording.
44. On Rodgers's use of scalar melodies throughout his career see Geoffrey Block, *Richard Rodgers* (New Haven, CT: Yale University Press), 34–35.
45. Mordaunt Hall, "Maurice Chevalier and Jeanette MacDonald in a Charming Romantic Musical Fantasy," *New York Times*, August 19, 1932, 20.
46. In the undated lyrics and music drafts housed in the Mamoulian Collection and the Conductor's Score (February 16) the lyric "than have her wed a commoner" sung in the film (and published *The Complete Lyrics of Lorenz Hart*, 176) was originally "than tell her she's a commoner." Rouben Mamoulian Collection, Library of Congress, Box 78, Folder 3 (Lyrics) and Box 78, Folder 4 (Music); Conductor's Score, Paramount Archives.
47. The Conductor's Score dated February 16 indicates that the first statement of "a tailor" uttered by Valentine in the film was originally intended for the First Aunt. The February score also

lists the Count's name as the actor [Roland] Young, who had not yet been replaced by Charles Butterworth.

48. The film replaces the Chef's lyric "I've given indigestion to the Prince of Wales, the Tsar and Queen Maria" with "I've given indigestion to a President, ptomaine to a Duke."

49. *The Complete Lyrics of Lorenz Hart*, 177.

50. Rouben Mamoulian Collection Box 78, Folder 3, Music and Lyrics (Lyrics 1932).

51. *The Complete Lyrics of Rodgers and Hart*, 176.

52. The song, recorded under the title "The Letter Song," can be heard sung by Lynn Redgrave and Arthur Siegel on *Ben Bagley's Rodgers and Hart Revisited Vol. III*. Painted Smiles Records PSCD-106 (1989).

53. *Love Me Tonight* Production Code Files, Correspondence 1931–1954, Margaret Herrick Library, Los Angeles.

54. The remnants of this scene can be found as early as the Synopsis when Maurice helps Nady (not yet Jeanette) with an arithmetic problem (6) and the Treatment when he helps Jeanette with a game of solitaire and they sing a song about it (Sequence C, 11). The Synopsis and the Treatment are both located in the Rouben Mamoulian Collection, Library of Congress, Box 79, Folder 4.

55. Rodgers underestimated the popularity of Paul Whiteman's recording of "Lover," which reached No. 3 on the *Billboard* charts for seven weeks in 1933, http:/www.tsort.info/music/yr1933 (accessed July 6, 2020). See note 6.

56. Rodgers recalled in his autobiography how "Louise" inspired "Mimi": "Chevalier had already done so well in immortalizing the charms of such ladies as Valentine and Louise that we decided to write a perky little piece for him about a girl named Mimi." Rodgers, *Musical Stages: An Autobiography* (New York: Da Capo, 1975), 151

57. "Dream Lover" sold 70,146 copies and "Beyond the Blue Horizon" 80,957. See Robbins, "Rescoring *Anything Goes* in 1930s Hollywood," 618 and note 2.

58. Ibid.

Chapter 3: Rodgers the Musical "Auteur": Instrumental Numbers, Leitmotivs, Borrowings, Allusions, and Underscoring

1. Richard Rodgers, *Musical Stages: An Autobiography* (New York: Random House, 1975), 149.

2. Ibid.

3. Paramount Archives, Music Archive, Paramount Pictures, Box 8489690. I am grateful to Annie Killelea at Paramount for making these scores available to me. I would also like to thank Dominic Broomfield-McHugh for calling my attention to the absence of Rodgers's musical notation in the Paramount materials listed as "handwritten score (R. Rodgers)."

4. Unlike many songwriters of his era Rodgers was a skilled musical technician and fully capable of writing leitmotivs and offering scoring suggestions for the "Hunt" and other instrumental numbers. He was also one of the relatively few composers who produced fair copies of his songs that "closely match the readily available published piano-vocal scores of these shows." Dominic McHugh, "'I'll Never Know Exactly Who Did What': Broadway Composers as Musical Collaborators," *Journal of the American Musicology Society* 68, no. 3 (Fall 2015): 605–52; quotation on 610.

5. It is also likely that Rodgers was *not* responsible for the opening and other details of the Prelude that went beyond the basic thematic material, the planning and synchronization of the March Maestoso (Majestic March), and other incidental music based on Rodgers's song melodies. The situation with *Love Me Tonight* might be similar to the working arrangement between Rodgers and his favored orchestrator, Robert Russell Bennett, on *Victory at Sea* twenty years later. With the latter work Rodgers composed twelve musical themes from which Bennett produced thirteen hours of orchestral music that found its way into a popular television documentary series about World War II naval operations that appeared on twenty-six half-hour broadcasts throughout the 1952–53 season.

6. "Myrna's Theme" (first page, mm. 1–8); "Duke Theme" (first page, mm. 9–10; second page, m. 1); "Aunts Theme" (second page, mm. 2–13); "Camera Theme" (mm. 13–18).

7. For a discussion of Verdi's treatment of the kiss theme see Richard Taruskin, *The Oxford History of Western Music*, Vol. 3: *The Nineteenth Century* (New York: Oxford University Press, 2003), 600–604 and 608–11.

8. For example, a "hate" theme embodied by the Jets in their gang whistle eventually metamorphoses into a "love" theme embodied in Maria's name in Tony's song "Maria."

9. "Myrna's Theme" vanishes after the Prelude, and the Count de Savignac is not assigned a leitmotiv (although when we hear a flute viewers might suspect he is in the neighborhood). In the case of Maurice and Jeanette, snippets of "Isn't It Romantic?" in the first part of the film and "Love Me Tonight" in the latter serve as their reminiscence themes (i.e., leitmotivs).

10. An eleventh borrowing, eight measures of "La Marseillaise," was removed from the completed film (see table 3.1 "Borrowings and Allusions").

11. Leipold composed the scores to hundreds of films from the late 1920s to the end of the 1950s. Before working on *Love Me Tonight* he had composed the scores for *Dr. Jekyll and Mr. Hyde* (1931), directed by Mamoulian, and *One Hour with You* (1932), which starred MacDonald and Chevalier, for director Ernst Lubitsch.

12. Perhaps Greig's most famous butler role was in Preston Sturges's *The Lady Eve* (1941), one of six Sturges films in which Greig was cast.

13. Rodgers, *Musical Stages*, 151.

14. By the time he drafted a complex and detailed version of the "awakening of Paris" in the Treatment (in which he invites comparison to a late scene in *Porgy*), Mamoulian was also referring to this scene as a "symphony of sounds." The Treatment (January 18) offers the most detailed description of the opening until the Release Dialogue Script in August.

15. Joseph Horowitz, *"On My Way": The Untold Story of Rouben Mamoulian, George Gershwin, and "Porgy and Bess"* (New York: W. W. Norton, 2013), 224–28. In the published play, which is divided into four acts, its placement corresponds to act 4, scene 3. Dorothy and DuBose Heyward, *Porgy: A Play in Four Acts* (New York: Doubleday, Doran, 1928); reprinted in *Famous American Plays of the 1920s and the 1930s* (Garden City, NY: The Fireside Theatre, 1988), 135–209.

16. Horowitz transcribed the "Symphony of Noises" text from *Porgy* from the Rouben Mamoulian Collection in the Library of Congress, Rouben Mamoulian Collection, Box 115, Folder 7. Before it was cut during the tryouts Mamoulian returned to the idea of a symphony of noises, five years after *Porgy* and three years after *Love Me Tonight*, to open the final scene of the opera *Porgy and Bess*, with lyrics by DuBose Heyward and Ira Gershwin and music by George Gershwin. This time Mamoulian called it the "Occupational Humoresque." In the recording with John Mauceri conducting the Nashville Symphony Orchestra it lasts a little over three minutes (Decca B0007431-02, 2 CDs, 2006). The "Occupational Humoresque" also appears in part in the 1959 Samuel Goldwyn film adaptation of *Porgy and Bess* directed by Otto Preminger, a film withdrawn by the Gershwin Estate since 1974. It's a reasonable, albeit unconfirmed, conjecture that the remnant of the "Occupational Humoresque" in the film may have been completed by Mamoulian before he was fired as director and replaced by Preminger.

17. Lea Jacobs, *Film Rhythm after Sound: Technology, Music, and Performance* (Oakland: University of California Press, 2015), 115–21.

18. Hannah Lewis, "*Love Me Tonight* (1932) and the Development of the Integrated Film Musical," *Musical Quarterly* 100, no. 1 (December 1, 2017), 11.

19. Andrew Sarris, ed., *Interviews with Film Directors* (Indianapolis, IN: Bobbs-Merrill, 1967), 290.

20. Until shot 18 all measures are in 4/4 time.

21. Jacobs's transcription precisely indicates the intricate rhythmic overlapping of cobblers 1 and 2.

22. Paul R. Hanson, *Historical Dictionary of the French Revolution* (Historical Dictionaries of War, Revolution, and Civil Unrest) (Lanham, MD: Rowman & Littlefield, 2nd ed. 2015), 53.

23. Rodgers's manuscript includes numerous instructions for the instrumentation, but only the Conductor's Score contains the scene directions.

24. Roger Hickman, *Reel Music: Exploring 100 Years of Film Music* (New York: W. W. Norton, 2006), 42.

25. Ibid., 119. Other examples of Mickey Mousing in *Love Me Tonight* include the glissando and cymbal crash heard when Count de Savignac falls off his ladder on his flute in the scene that directly followed "Isn't It Romantic?" and the *pizzicato* sounds that imitate Jeanette's heartbeat and pulse during her examination by the Doctor in "A Woman Needs Something Like That." Both of these examples are described and designated Mickey Mousing in Michael Slowik, *After the Silents: Hollywood Film Music in the Early Sound Era, 1926–1935* (New York: Columbia University Press, 2014), 171–72.

26. Technically, the deer being hunted is a stag (i.e., an adult male deer as opposed to a doe [a deer] a female deer), but this chapter will use Rodgers's term and refer to the animal that Maurice rescues from the hunt as a deer throughout.

27. Rodgers, *Musical Stages,* 149.
28. Conductor's Score: "Pastorale" (page 2, system 2); "The Hunt" (page 2, system 3); and "La Sortie de L'eau" (page 8, system 3).
29. A few years earlier Rodgers had also quoted from another ballet for humorous purposes. In the middle of the triumphal march from *Chee-Chee* (1928), in which the Grand Eunuch is about to be castrated (yes, *Chee-Chee* was a 1920s musical comedy), Rodgers "inserted several bars of Tchaikovsky's *Nutcracker Suite*" (Rodgers, *Musical Stages,* 119). Rodgers "found it gratifying that at almost every performance [31 total] there were two or three individuals with ears musically sharp enough to appreciate the joke" (Ibid.).
30. In 1960 "Walking the Dog" was published as an independent instrumental piece called "Promenade."
31. Gershwin noted the completion of eight *Damsel* songs in a letter to his first biographer, Isaac Goldberg, on May 12, 1937, and a ninth and final song in a May 17 letter to his cousin and business assistant, Henry Botkin. For the May 12 letter see Edward Jablonski and Lawrence D. Stewart, *The Gershwin Years* (Garden City, NY: Doubleday, 1973), 276; for the May 17 letter see Robert Wyatt and John Andrew Johnson, eds., *The George Gershwin Reader* (New York: Oxford University Press, 2004), 261. The Script Files housed among the *Damsel in Distress* Production Files, UCLA, RKO Collection, Box 527S, reveals that the *Damsel* screenplay was mainly written in July and completed in late September, more than two months after George's unexpected death on July 11 (shooting took place between July 22 and October 16, and the screenplay is dated September 25). For more on the compositional process of *Damsel in Distress* see Geoffrey Block, "When Fred Lost Ginger: Thoughts on the Genesis and Legacy of *A Damsel in Distress* (RKO 1937)," in *The Oxford Handbook of the Hollywood Musical,* ed. Dominic Broomfield-McHugh (New York: Oxford University Press, 2022).

Chapter 4: Sex and Censorship

1. From 1934 to 1954 Joseph I. Breen headed the Production Code Administration (PCA) in charge of enforcing and administering the Motion Picture Production Code. See note 27 concerning the reference to the Hays Code.
2. Memo from Joseph I. Breen to Luigi Luraschi, September 26, 1949, *Love Me Tonight,* Production Code Files, Correspondence 1931–1954, Margaret Herrick Library, Los Angeles.
3. See Mark A. Vieira, *Sin in Soft Focus: Pre-Code Hollywood* (New York: Harry N. Abrams, 1999), 99, and Mark A. Vieira, *Forbidden Hollywood: The Pre-Code Era (1930–1934)* (Philadelphia: Running Press, 2019), 153.
4. James Kotsilibars-Davis and Myrna Loy, *Myrna Loy: Being and Becoming* (New York: Knopf, 1987), 124. The photo of Myrna Loy cut from the negative in connection with the 1949 rerelease shown in Figure 4.1 was printed in Vieira, *Sin in Soft Focus,* 99, and reprinted in Vieira, *Forbidden Hollywood,* 153. In the photo Loy is sitting up at the edge of her bed singing or about to sing her snippet of melody from her deleted portion of the "Mimi" reprise.
5. The Code has been reprinted in a number of sources. The source used in this chapter is the Appendix to Doherty, *Hollywood's Censor,* 351–63.
6. According to Vieira, "from all available evidence, the term 'Pre-Code' was first applied by a repertory film programmer named Bruce Goldstein," who coined the term in 1988 (Vieira, *Forbidden Hollywood,* 8, 251).
7. Two of Mamoulian's films that preceded *Love Me Tonight* also experienced a troubled rerelease history and were also withdrawn from circulation soon after the Production Code began to be more rigorously enforced in 1934. The petition to rerelease *City Streets* (1931), a pioneering gangster film notable for its conspicuous absence of on-screen violence, was rejected in 1936, and *Dr. Jekyll and Mr. Hyde,* which "passed virtually without incident" in 1931, ran into censorship trouble in 1935 on account of an "the undressing scene that had passed the review board" upon its initial release (Spergel, *Reinventing Reality,* 116, 125). As with *Love Me Tonight* some material from *Dr. Jekyll* was excised, the film was withdrawn from circulation, and it wasn't until 1992 that the missing scenes were located and restored and made available for viewing (David Luhrssen, *Mamoulian: Life on Stage and Screen* (Lexington, KY: University Press of Kentucky, 2013), 59). Meanwhile the missing material from *Love Me Tonight* remains missing other than the still photograph of Myrna Loy shown in Figure 4.1.

8. *Love Me Tonight,* Production Code Files, Correspondence 1931–1954, Margaret Herrick Library, Los Angeles. Unless otherwise noted all future communications between Paramount and the SRC are located in these files. The recipients and dates are provided in the main text.
9. Vieira, *Forbidden Hollywood,* 24.
10. Leonard J. Leff and Jerold L. Simmons, *The Dame in the Kimono: Hollywood, Censorship, and the Production Code from the 1920s to the 1960s* (New York: Grove Weidenfeld, 1990), 15.
11. Not surprisingly, "thank God" was not yet crossed out in the Conductor's Score dated January 21, one day *before* Lasky sent the lyric to Joy. Conductor's Score, Paramount Archives, Music Archives, Paramount Pictures.
12. Dorothy Hart and Robert Kimball, eds., *The Complete Lyrics of Lorenz Hart* (New York: Knopf, 1985; expanded ed. New York: Da Capo, 1995), 171.
13. Along with "The Poor Apache" Lasky also sent two copies of what he referred to as "the second script" and what Joy referred to as "the revised script." Since Lasky had sent "the first buff script" (which we have earlier identified more simply as the "Buff Script") on March 26 and had not yet sent "the first white script" (i.e., the "White Script" dated April 19), the Lasky–Joy correspondence raises the possibility of an intermediate script between March 26 and April 19 that is no longer extant. The White Script, discussed in chapter 1, is located in the Mamoulian Collection, Box 79, Folder 2, Library of Congress, Washington, DC. See also Table 1.1.
14. The Buff Script (March 26), which preceded the White Script (April 19), is located in the Mamoulian Collection, Box 79, Folder 1, Library of Congress, Washington, DC (see chapter 1).
15. Joy's reasons for removing these French ethnic references are worth noting. He believed that the Royalists "would object to being shown striking inferious [inferiors], and the Republicans to the fact that a French citizen would submit to such an insult."
16. The reference to the 14th of July appears on scene B-48 of the Buff Script (main page B-18). The final screenplay also includes a reference to the storming of the Bastille prior to Maurice's decision to go to the chateau and get the Vicomte to pay for his newly tailored suits. The Shirtmaker wants "to get a crowd, march down there, and attack that chateau," but Maurice decides to do this alone as "a one-man French Revolution." Not only was "Your Highness" retained in the White Script, it also appeared in the final screenplay and film.
17. The Production Code, see Doherty, *Hollywood's Censor,* 354.
18. April 20, 1932, memo from Lamar Trotti to Jesse Lasky, *Love Me Tonight,* Production Code Files, Correspondence 1931–1954, Margaret Herrick Library, Los Angeles.
19. In the same memo Fisher includes a message designed for foreign offices: "The treatment of the French should occasion no difficulty although there is one mention of Rochambeau in connection with the Princess's first husband. It is indicated both in the dialogue and by the insert of a photo that this Rochambeau was far too old to do her any good." The presumed ancestor of Jeanette's husband, "a Rochambeau," is Jean-Baptiste Donatien de Vimeur, comte de Rochambeau, who died in 1807 and who, along with fellow Frenchman Lafayette, played a major role in defeating the British during the American Revolution. If he's unfamiliar to modern viewers, it might be because, while his name occurs in two references in the musical *Hamilton* (2015), "Guns and Ships" and "Yorktown," he does not appear as a character. This is probably opportunity to also state that no persuasive extant evidence supports the rumor that Rochambeau was the inventor of the game rock, paper, scissors, widely referred to as roshambo.
20. Doherty, *Hollywood's Censor,* 32–33. In 1952 the US Supreme Court reversed its 1915 decision and granted films First Amendment protections (Ibid., 302–3).
21. Ibid., 33.
22. Vieira, *Forbidden Hollywood,* 21.
23. Leff and Simmons, *The Dame in the Kimono,* 11.
24. Quoted in Doherty, *Hollywood's Censor,* 172.
25. Leff and Simmons, *The Dame in the Kimono,* 8.
26. Doherty, *Hollywood's Censor,* 79.
27. Leff and Simmons, *The Dame in the Kimono,* 59. Will H. Hays was Chairman of the MPPDA from 1922 to 1945. Although he played an indispensable role in the development of the film industry, the original Code in 1930 was written by the influential Catholics Martin S. Quigley and Father Daniel Lord. When people commonly started referring to the Code as the "Hays Code," however, Hays embraced and perpetuated the error. Eventually the name "Hays Code" gained common currency and remains widely used in the literature about the Production Code and film history.

28. Richard Barrios speculates that Paramount's desire to reissue *Love Me Tonight* was motivated by the current popularity of the early films in Jeanette MacDonald's MGM operetta series with Nelson Eddy, *Naughty Marietta* (1935) and *Rose Marie* (released in January 1936). Barrios, *A Song in the Dark: The Birth of the Musical Film* (New York: Oxford University Press, 1995; 2nd ed., 2010), 352.

29. Doherty, *Hollywood's Censor*, 352.

30. *Guilty as Hell*, a mystery film, released days before *Love Me Tonight* on August 5, 1932, was not included among the eleven pictures under discussion between Paramount and the PCA during the previous four months.

31. Breen's only objection to *Guilty as Hell* expressed in the January 20 memo was its attempt to circumvent the untenable hypothesis that "crime pays by allowing the criminal to escape justice by committing suicide." Although the main authors of the original Code in 1930, Quigley and Father Lord, had inexplicably neglected to include suicide as a sin, Breen (like Quigley and Lord a devout Catholic) followed doctrine on this issue, even before suicide was formally "discouraged as morally questionable and as bad theatre" in a 1938 Code resolution. In 1951 the Code was amended to clarify that this morally questionable act "should never be justified or glorified or used to defeat the due process of law." Doherty, *Hollywood's Censor*, 355.

32. Geoffrey Shurlock served on the PCA since 1934 and would eventually succeed Breen as its director from 1954 until the demise of the PCA in 1968. That same year the PCA was replaced by the Motion Picture Association of America (MPAA) ratings system. The main ratings at present are: G = General Release; PG = Parental Guidance Suggested; PG-13 = Parents Strongly Cautioned; R = Restricted; NC-17 = Adults Only. Had *Love Me Tonight* been first issued after 1968, it probably would have received a PG, but if those assigning the rating understood the film according to Breen's way of thinking, it might have earned a PG-13.

33. In his only correction in the memo, Shurlock had originally written "as a matter of fact" before crossing out the word "fact" and replacing it with "record."

34. In the October 25 memo Breen also offered a certificate to authorize the release of Lubitsch's *One Hour with You* (1931), the previous Chevalier–MacDonald film released in March 1932, directed by Lubitsch.

35. Geoffrey Block, *Richard Rodgers* (New Haven, CT: Yale University Press, 2003), 159.

36. Leff and Simmons, *The Dame in the Kimono*, 194.

37. The Catholic Legion of Decency was the organization that supported the Catholic response to the perceived low morality of Hollywood films. It was founded in November 1933 to provide a united front that could boycott unsavory films and enforce the Code. When in May 1934 one of its leaders, Cardinal Dougherty of Philadelphia, demanded that his diocese "boycott *all* motion pictures" the response was that "box-office receipts immediately fell 40 percent," a development that perhaps more than any other paved the way for the adoption of the PCA in July that same year.

38. Doherty, *Hollywood's Censor*, 352.

39. See chapter 2 for a discussion of the words and music and singing vs. speaking in "A Woman Needs Something Like That."

40. As rereleased, the final suggestive words of the Doctor are, "With eyes and red lips / And a figure like that!/You're not wasted away—/You're just wasted." The deleted stanza with lines such as "A flower needs sprinkling" and "a peach must be eaten" were printed in *The Complete Lyrics of Lorenz Hart*, 175.

41. The author has found examples of officially censored material in nearly every film in which he has had an opportunity to see the censor reports in the production files at the Margaret Herrick Library in Los Angeles and other collections such as the Library of Congress. In all these files, an almost ubiquitous proviso in PSA directives is that "the final judgment will be based on the finished picture." To take an example again from the film adaptation of *South Pacific* in the Shurlock era of the PCA, according to correspondence preserved in the Joshua Logan papers in the Library of Congress, Shurlock insisted on the removal of Luther Billis's suggestive description delivered in an "evil" tone about the boar's tooth ceremonial on Bali Ha'i. Although Twentieth Century-Fox gave the impression of complying by removing Luther's offending words (and description of his tone) from the screenplay, both the lines and their suggestive delivery remained in the final film for posterity. Block, *Richard Rodgers*, 158. To say that the Code was not foolproof would be a colossal understatement.

42. Vieira, *Forbidden Hollywood*, 221.

43. Tennessee Williams scholar Gene D. Phillips discusses the compromise reached between Breen and Williams: "Stanley [Kowalski, played by Marlon Brando] had to be punished for his lust, even though there is a strong possibility that Blanche was at least subconsciously responsible for encouraging him to seduce her. The ending of the film was revised, therefore, to give the impression that Stella was leaving Stanley by having her say to her newborn infant, 'We're not going back in there. Not this time. We're never going back.' This was a shrewdly ambiguous way to end the movie, since the unsophisticated could believe that Stella would make good her resolution. The more mature viewer, however, would realize that Stella had left Stanley earlier in the film in the wake of a domestic brawl, and returned to him when he begged her forgiveness; and there is ample reason to believe that she will do so again." Phillips, *The Films of Tennessee Williams* (London: Associated University Presses, 1980), 84–85.

44. Maurice even announces the verdict (34 inches) in passing as he hums the melody of "Isn't It Romantic?" A photograph of Chevalier measuring Jeanette's bust taken directly from the film has been frequently reprinted, including in this volume. (see Figure 4.2).

45. Miles Kreuger, Audio Commentary, *Love Me Tonight*, Kino Video K322 (2003).

46. Later in the film the wife of Pierre, who drives Maurice to the chateau to collect payment from Gilbert, projects a romantic interest toward Maurice entirely through her body language.

47. Rick Altman, *The American Film Musical* (Bloomington: Indiana University Press, 1989), 150–58.

48. Ibid., 155.

49. Ibid., 155–56.

50. In the early twenty-first century, the sentiments of Jeanette's doctor and Rhett Butler remain evident in the pilot to the Japanese Manga series *Yu-Gi-Oh! The Abridged Series* (Season 1, Episode 1, July 14, 2006). In this opening episode the frequent trope about the need for sexual release is expressed directly (and coarsely) by an unfiltered character (the Grandfather) who emphatically asserts, "That Kaiba kid needs to get laid."

51. Altman, *The American Film Musical*, 157.

52. Ibid., 159.

53. Ralph Williams, "New Chevalier Film Tribute to Direction," *Rochester Journal*, September 9, 1932. Mamoulian Collection, Library of Congress, "Press Reviews 1932–33," Box 78, Folder 6.

Chapter 5: The Reception of *Love Me Tonight* from Its Time to Ours

1. Bradley, *The First Hollywood Musicals*, 297. The two moneymakers were Lubitsch's *One Hour with You* and *The Big Broadcast* starring Bing Crosby.

2. Bradley considers *Horse Feathers* and *Dancers in the Dark* to be "borderline" musicals (Ibid.).

3. Mordaunt Hall, "Maurice Chevalier and Jeanette MacDonald in a Charming Romantic Fantasy," *New York Times*, August 19, 1932. René Clair's name used to arise almost invariably as an important influence on Mamoulian, who was well acquainted with Clair's films (and even Clair himself at least when they were allegedly childhood classmates at the Lycée Montaigne in Paris). In both editions of *A Song in the Dark* Barrios singles out Clair's "rapid-fire rhythmic editing and passing lyrics from one person to the next," both evident in *Sous Les Toits de Paris (On the Roofs of Paris)* (1930), as Clair techniques, but only in the first edition does he state that Mamoulian's passed-along song "Isn't It Romantic?" owes anything to Clair. Curiously, the paragraph containing this reference to "Isn't It Romantic?" was the only one that did *not* resurface in the second edition (Barrios, *A Song in the Dark*, 1st ed., 358 [quote] and 360 [Clair influence]; 2nd ed., 345 [quote]). Mark Spergel's comprehensive study of Mamoulian mentions Clair only once and somewhat dismissively: "Some critics have claimed that *Love Me Tonight* is derivative of Rene [René] Clair's film *Sous Les Toits de Paris,* especially in its opening sequence. Whatever resemblance it bears to the Clair film, the opening is a near replication of the early morning awakening scene of Catfish row in *Porgy*." Mark Spergel, *Reinventing Reality—The Art and Life of Rouben Mamoulian* (Metuchen, NJ; Scarecrow, 1993), 131. In the most recent Mamoulian biography as of this writing, Clair is not mentioned even once. David Luhrssen, *Mamoulian on Stage and Screen* (Lexington: University of Kentucky Press, 2013).

4. E.W. B, "Maurice Chevalier and Jeanette MacDonald Version of 'The Sleeping Beauty,'" *The Era* (London), November 23, 1932. The name Disney might appear somewhat prescient since the first Disney feature film, *Snow White and the Seven Dwarfs,* was still six years in the future.

5. William F. McDermott, "Chevalier Film from the Stage Point of View," *Cleveland Plain Dealer*, September 7, 1932.

6. Richard E. Hays, "Chevalier Film One of Screen's Real Triumphs," *Seattle Times*, September 2, 1932.

7. Quoted in Horowitz, *"On My Way": The Untold Story of Rouben Mamoulian, George Gershwin, and "Porgy and Bess"* (New York: W. W. Norton, 2013), 102.

8. *Variety* on May 30, 1932, adds that the over-budget expenses of *Love Me Tonight* were due mainly to the fact that *both* Chevalier and MacDonald had to be paid weekly during the screenwriting as well as the shooting and "that Paramount was compelled to buy up several theatre dates Chevalier had in Europe for personal appearances." "Chevalier's 'Love Me' Runs Beyond Million Cost," *Variety*, May 30, 1932.

9. According to Altman, *Love Me Tonight* "remains one of the few films of the period still regularly screened and admired today." Rick Altman, *The American Film Musical* (Bloomington: Indiana University Press, 1987), 150. In Altman's defense, since *Love Me Tonight* was not widely screened in 1987 when he published his study, Altman is likely referring to the film's impact on scholars, critics, film directors, and other industry professionals rather than the general public who would not for the most part get an opportunity to admire this film until its 2003 release.

10. Kurt Weill, "Music in the Movies," *Harper's Bazaar* 80, no. 9 (September 1946), 257, 398, 400), quotation on 400; reprinted in Lewis Jacobs, ed., *The Movies as Medium* (New York: Farrar, Straus and Giroux, 1970), 289–96.

11. John Kobal, *Gotta Sing, Gotta Dance: A Pictorial History of Film Musicals* (London: Hamlyn, 1971; rev. ed., London: Spring, 1988), 204. Minnelli's biographer Emanuel Levy writes that Minnelli liked the way Mamoulian "interweaved cleverly the Rodgers and Hart songs into the story" and "particularly liked Mamoulian's treatment of one number, 'The Son-of-a-Gun Is Nothing but a Tailor,'" and the effective denouement." Levy, *Vincente Minnelli: Hollywood's Dark Dreamer* (New York: St. Martin's, 2009), 56–57.

12. Jeanine Basinger describes this opening as a "tribute to the opening of Mamoulian's *Love Me Tonight*," not only with its opening aerial view of Paris but also the way it introduces the central characters, Chevalier and Gene Kelly, respectively), adding that "if an audience doesn't know that, it doesn't matter." Basinger, *The Movie Musical!* (New York: Knopf, 2019), 469.

13. Ibid., 140.

14. Aljean Harmetz, *The Making of "The Wizard of Oz"* (New York: Knopf, 1977), 85.

15. Hugh Fordin, *M-G-M's Greatest Musicals: The Arthur Freed Unit* (New York: Da Capo, 1996), 185.

16. Emily Anderson, trans. and ed., *The Letters of Mozart and His Family, Volume II* (New York: Macmillan, 1966), 800. This was the same Swieten who shared his knowledge of Bach and Handel with Haydn and who wrote the librettos for both *The Creation* and *The Seasons*.

17. Daniel Heartz, *Mozart, Haydn and Early Beethoven 1781–1802* (New York: W. W. Norton, 2009), 678.

18. Among Mamoulian's sixteen films from 1929 to 1957, four are unequivocally musicals: *Love Me Tonight* (1932); *High, Wide and Handsome*, screenplay and lyrics by Oscar Hammerstein and music by Jerome Kern (1937); *Summer Holiday*, lyrics by Ralph Blane and music by Harry Warren; and *Silk Stockings*, lyrics and music by Cole Porter. Although Mamoulian's film debut, *Applause* (1929), contains only two featured songs, it is usually treated as a musical in books on musicals; on the other hand, *The Gay Desperado* (1936), which contains three songs, is rarely grouped under the film musical rubric. Without explanation, Jeanine Basinger sides with the minority in *The Movie Musical!* 61.

19. Mark Grant, *The Rise and Fall of the Broadway Musical* (Boston: Northeastern University Press, 2004), 239.

20. Andrew Sarris, *The American Cinema: Directors and Directions 1929–1968* (New York: Dutton, 1968; rev. ed., New York: Da Capo, 1996), 161.

21. Ibid. A few years later Sarris compared Mamoulian unfavorably with Lubitsch when he wrote that he "would not trade Lubitsch's daringly subdued and scintillatingly circular treatment of 'The Merry Widow Waltz' as a prison-cell *pas-de-deux* for all the showy camera angles in LOVE ME TONIGHT." Sarris, "Lubitsch in the Thirties: All Talking! All Singing! All Lubitsch!" *Film Comment* 8, no. 2 (Summer 1972), 21.

22. David Thomson, *The New Biographical Dictionary of Film* (New York: Knopf, 2002), 556.

23. Richard Barrios, *Dangerous Rhythm: Why Movie Musicals Matter* (New York: Oxford University Press, 2014), 173n1.

24. Leonard Maltin, *Turner Classic Movies Present Leonard Maltin's Classic Movie Guide: From the Silent Era through 1965*, 3rd ed. (New York: Plume, 2015), 410; Barrios, *A Song in the Dark*, 347–48.

25. Gene Ringgold and Dewitt Bodeen, *Chevalier*, 110. Unfortunately, Ringgold and Bodeen are quoting John Baxter verbatim here. See John Baxter, *Hollywood in the Thirties* (New York: Paperback Library, 1970), 61.

26. Basinger, *The Movie Musical!* 69.

27. Tom Milne, *Rouben Mamoulian* (Bloomington: Indiana University Press, 1969), 51.

28. Baxter, *Hollywood in the Thirties*, 60.

29. Bradley, *The First Hollywood Musicals*, 306.

30. *A Love Parade*: Victor Schertzinger (music) and Clifford Grey (lyrics); *Monte Carlo*: Richard A. Whiting and W. Franke Harling (music) and Leo Robin (lyrics); *The Smiling Lieutenant*: Oscar Straus (music) and Grey (lyrics); and *One Hour with You*: Straus (music) and Robin (lyrics).

31. Barrios, *A Song in the Dark: The Birth of the Musical Film* (New York: Oxford University Press, 1995; 2nd ed., 2010), 360.

32. James Harvey, *Romantic Comedy in Hollywood, from Lubitsch to Sturges* (New York: Knopf, 1987), 31. Despite the commentary in this chapter that favors Mamoulian at the expense of Lubitsch, it would be remiss to neglect or dismiss the magnitude of Lubitsch's overall historical and artistic importance and beyond the four pioneering and brilliant film musicals he directed between 1929 and 1934, including the acclaimed nonmusical *Trouble in Paradise* in 1932, the same year as *Love Me Tonight*, and *Design for Living* one year later. Before 1929, and long before Mamoulian's first movie, Lubitsch had been a leading director in Germany and had directed over fifty silent films. One of these films, *The Marriage Circle* from 1924 (remade as the musical *One Hour with You*), has been described as "a model of sophisticated comedy for the silent era" (Thomson, *The New Biographical Dictionary of Film*, 536). In the years that followed his final musical, *The Merry Widow*, Lubitsch went on to direct movies for another thirteen years before his death in 1946, including some of the most highly regarded American films of any era: *Ninotchka* (1939), *The Shop Around the Corner* (1940), *To Be or Not to Be* (1942), and *Heaven Can Wait* (1943). His productivity and range are enormous, surpassing even Mamoulian in his influence and overall impact.

33. Kennedy, *Roadshow!* 6.

34. Ibid.

35. Jesse Green, "Sondheim Dismembers 'Sweeney' and 'Back Story,'" *New York Times*, December 16, 2007.

36. Robert Sokol, Ken Kwartier, and Terri Roberts, "Side by Side: Rich and Sondheim," *The Sondheim Review* 15, no. 1 (Fall 2008): 22–24. Since I was present at this interview, I can report more precisely that Sondheim was basing this judgment on personal experience when he said that *Sweeney* was "the most satisfying version of a stage piece I've ever seen."

37. Green, "Sondheim Dismembers 'Sweeney.'"

38. The other two are *Under the Roofs of Paris (Sous les Toits de Paris)* (1930), directed by René Clair, and *The Smiling Lieutenant* (1931), directed by Lubitsch and starring Chevalier.

39. Bruce Beresford, "Introduction," in John Simon, *John Simon on Film: Criticism, 1982–2001* (New York: Applause Theatre & Cinema Books, 2005), 5.

Appendix 1

1. Most of the information in this table, including dates, is provided curtesy of Wikipedia and the Internet Movie Database (IMDb). The master list of cast members was taken from the 2003 DVD (Kino K322), where with the exceptions of Thomas Rickett's birth year (1852) and more dramatically the birth year of Ethel Wales (the Dressmaker Mme. Dutoit) (1898), the dates match with Wikipedia and the IMDb.

Appendix 2

1. When the doctor introduces himself as "Doctor Pierre de Pontignac, a noble family, and now I'm at my ease" (right before he asks Jeanette to remove her dress), his speech is underscored by the first eight measures of "La Marseillaise."

Selected Bibliography

Altman, Rick. *The American Film Musical.* Bloomington: Indiana University Press, 1987.

Banks, Adrian. "Rouben Mamoulian." *Senses of Cinema* 42, no. 42 (February 2007): 1–28. http://sensesofcinema.com/2007/great-directors/mamoulian/ (accessed on September 12, 2018.

Barrios, Richard. *A Song in the Dark: The Birth of the Musical Film.* New York: Oxford University Press, 1995; 2nd ed. 2010.

Barrios, Richard. *Dangerous Rhythm: Why Movie Musicals Matter.* New York: Oxford University Press, 2014.

Barrios, Richard. "*Love Me Tonight.*" Library of Congress. http://loc.gov/static/programs/national-film-preservation-board/documents/love_me_tonight.pdf (accessed on November 20, 2019).

Basinger, Jeanine. *The Movie Musical!* New York: Knopf, 2019.

Behr, Edward. *The Good Frenchman: The True Story of the Life and Times of Maurice Chevalier.* New York: Villard Books, 1993.

Block, Geoffrey. *Richard Rodgers.* New Haven, CT: Yale University Press, 2003.

Bradley, Edwin M. *The First Hollywood Musical: A Critical Filmography of 171 Features, 1927 through 1932.* Jefferson, NC: McFarland, 1996.

Doherty, Thomas. *Hollywood's Censor: Joseph I. Breen and the Production Code Administration.* New York: Columbia University Press, 2007.

Feuer, Jane. *The Hollywood Musical.* Bloomington: Indiana University Press, 1982; expanded ed. 1993.

Fordin, Hugh. *M-G-M's Greatest Musicals: The Arthur Freed Unit.* New York: Da Capo, 1996.

Genné, Beth. *Dance Me a Song: Astaire, Balanchine, Kelly, and the American Film Musical.* New York: Oxford University Press, 2018.

Hall, Mordaunt. "Maurice Chevalier and Jeanette MacDonald in a Charming Romantic Musical Fantasy." *New York Times,* August 19, 1932, 20.

Hanke, Ken. "Rouben Mamoulian." *Films in Review* 38, nos. 8–9 (August–September 1988): 403–13.

Hart, Dorothy, and Robert Kimball, eds. *The Complete Lyrics of Lorenz Hart.* New York: Knopf, 1985; expanded ed. New York: Da Capo, 1995.

Harvey, James. *Romantic Comedy in Hollywood, from Lubitsch to Sturgis.* New York: Knopf, 1987.

Hingham, Charles, and Joel Greenberg, eds. *The Celluloid Muse: Hollywood Directors Speak.* London: Angus and Robertson, 1969.

Horowitz, Joseph. *"On My Way": The Untold Story of Rouben Mamoulian, George Gershwin, and "Porgy and Bess."* New York: W. W. Norton, 2013.

Jacobs, Lea. "The Innovation of Re-Recording in the Hollywood Studios." *Film History* 24 (2012): 5–34.

Jacobs, Lea. *Film Rhythm after Sound: Technology, Music, and Performances.* Oakland: University of California Press, 2015.

Kobal, John. *Gotta Sing, Gotta Dance: A Pictorial History of Film Musicals.* London: Hamlyn, 1971; rev. ed., London: 1988.

Kotsilibas-Davies, James, and Myrna Loy. *Being and Becoming.* New York: Knopf, 1987.

Kreuger, Miles. Audio Commentary, *Love Me Tonight,* Kino Video K322 (2003).

Leff, Leonard J., and Jerold L. Simmons. *The Dame in the Kimono: Hollywood, Censorship, and the Production Code from the 1920s to the 1960s.* New York: Anchor Books, Doubleday, 1990.

Lewis, Hannah. "*Love Me Tonight* (1932) and the Development of the Integrated Film Musical." *Musical Quarterly* 100, no. 1 (December 2017): 1–40.

McBride, Joseph. *How Did Lubitsch Do It?* New York: Columbia University Press, 2018.

Marmorstein, Gary. *A Ship without a Sail: The Life of Lorenz Hart.* New York: Simon & Schuster, 2012.

Milne, Tom. *Mamoulian.* Bloomington: Indiana University Press, 1969.

Mordden, Ethan. *When Broadway Went to Hollywood.* New York: Oxford University Press, 2016.

Nolan, Frederick. *Lorenz Hart: A Poet on Broadway.* New York: Oxford University Press, 1994.

Ringgold, Gene, and Dewitt Bodden. *Chevalier: The Films and Career of Maurice Chevalier.* Secaucus, NJ: The Citadel Press, 1973.

Robbins, Allison. "Rescoring *Anything Goes* in 1930s Hollywood," in *The Oxford Handbook of Musical Theatre Screen Adaptations,* ed. Dominic McHugh. New York: Oxford University Press, 2019.

Rodgers, Richard. *Musical Stages: An Autobiography.* New York: Random House, 1975.

Rodgers, Richard. *Richard Rodgers: Letters to Dorothy,* ed. William W. Appleton. New York: New York Public Library, 1988.

Secrest, Meryle. *Somewhere for Me: A Biography of Richard Rodgers.* New York: Knopf, 2001.

Silke, James R., ed. *Rouben Mamoulian: Style Is the Man.* Los Angeles: Center for Advanced Film Studies, 1971.

Slowik, Michael. *After the Silents: Hollywood Film Music in the Early Sound Era, 1926–1932.* New York: Columbia University Press, 2014.

Spergel, Mark. *The Art and Life of Rouben Mamoulian.* Metuchen, NJ: Scarecrow, 1993.

Symonds, Dominic. *We'll Have Manhattan: The Early Work of Rodgers and Hart.* New York: Oxford University Press, 2015.

Thomson, David. *The New Biographical Dictionary of Film.* New York: Knopf, 2002.

Turk, Edward Baron. *Hollywood Diva: A Biography of Jeanette MacDonald.* Berkeley: University of California Press, 1998.

Vieira, Mark A. *Forbidden Hollywood, The Pre-Code Era (1930–1934): When Sin Ruled the Movies.* Philadelphia: Running Press, 2019.

Weill, Kurt. "Music in the Movies." *Harper's Bazaar* 80, no. 9 (September 1946): 257, 398, 400; reprinted in Jacobs, Lewis, ed. *The Movies as Medium.* New York: Farrar, Straus and Giroux, 1970), 289–96.

Wilder, Alec. *American Popular Music: The Great Innovators, 1900–1950.* New York: Oxford University Press, 1972.

Index

For the benefit of digital users, indexed terms that span two pages (e.g., 52–53) may, on occasion, appear on only one of those pages.

Musical examples, figures, and tables are indicated by an italic *m*, *f*, and *t* following the page number.